★ ★ ★ ★ ★ ★ ★

DRAMATIC

SUCCESS!

★ ★ ★ ★ ★ ★ ★

DRAMATIC SUCCESS!

Theatre techniques to transform and inspire your working life

Andrew Leigh & Michael Maynard

NICHOLAS BREALEY
PUBLISHING

LONDON
YARMOUTH, MAINE

First published by
Nicholas Brealey Publishing in 2004

3–5 Spafield Street
Clerkenwell, London
EC1R 4QB, UK
Tel: +44 (0)20 7239 0360
Fax: +44 (0)20 7239 0370

PO Box 700
Yarmouth
Maine 04096, USA
Tel: (888) BREALEY
Fax: (207) 846 5181

http://www.nbrealey-books.com
http://www.maynardleigh.co.uk

ISBN 1-85788-340-3

British Library Cataloguing in Publication Data
A catalogue record for this book is available from the British Library.

Library of Congress Cataloging-in-Publication Data
Leigh, Andrew.
    Dramatic success! : theatre techniques to transform and inspire
your working life / Andrew Leigh & Michael Maynard.
        p. cm.
    Includes index.
    ISBN 1-85788-340-3
    1. Success in business. 2. Creative ability in business. 3. Employee
motivation. 4. Teams in the workplace. 5. Organizational
effectiveness. 6. Theater--Production and direction. I. Title: Theatre
techniques to transform and inspire your working life.
II. Maynard, Michael. III. Title.

HF5386.L553 2004
650.1--dc22

2003065403

Printed in Finland by WS Bookwell.

CONTENTS

★ ★ ★ ★ ★

★ ★ ★ ★ ★

CONTENTS

BOX OFFICE

What sort of ticket do you want for your performance at work? One for improving your own potential, one for creating a great team, or perhaps one for developing leadership? Maybe you want one of the expensive seats, one that will help produce an outstanding company?

The world of the performing arts is a world of vision, spirit and vitality. Performers can move and inspire you, help you understand complex aspects of life and even touch your soul. Above all, performance is about transformation. This is seldom by pure chance. It's a theatrical norm to strive for exceptional rather than ordinary performance. And, of course, the best of corporate life can be just as exciting and inspiring.

We have always been fascinated by what makes for outstanding performance. Before launching Maynard Leigh Associates (MLA) in 1989, Michael worked as a professional actor, writer and theatre director for nearly 20 years. Meanwhile Andrew was a senior executive, managing a cast of many hundreds, having been a business journalist and later a business book author. In our varied roles we sometimes encountered extraordinary performances, whether in the theatre or the corporate world. Occasionally we were even fortunate enough to be part of these experiences ourselves. This book explores what it takes to create and develop such brilliant performances.

MLA has pioneered the use of theatre techniques in business to create better performance. It is impossible to start this book without referring to our own dramatic story. We have grown a company and created a community dedicated to unlocking the potential of individuals, teams and organizations. We've won the occasional award along the way. Our clients have included HP, Vodafone, Campbells, Lloyds TSB, Visa, Carlsberg-Tetley, London Stock Exchange, and other equally illustrious names. Throughout we have tried hard to practise what we preach, by creating an organization that attracts and retains the most talented people who are passionate about investing their energy and spirit.

While steering MLA we threatened our work–life balance by also writing books on communication, presentation, leadership, teams and other management issues. This forced us to question the way that many businesses work, including our own. We have sought to identify what allows them to perform at their best. What you are reading distils our learning and ideas into a holistic view of how you can dramatically change your organization and improve your own and other people's performance.

Yet it remains work in progress. We are still in the middle of our performance, continuing to rewrite, rehearse and refine what happens on stage. Our clients naturally constitute a tough audience and we're continually challenged to do better. We are happy to share our experiences here. You have your ticket, now enjoy the show.

Andrew Leigh & Michael Maynard
October 2003

STAGE DIRECTIONS

Playwrights provide written instructions on what should happen during a stage performance. These are suggestions on when or where some action should occur or clarification on logistics.

You will find the equivalent of stage directions in this book: tips, ideas, experiences and exercises that we use with clients, and that you might find of value in your own workplace. They are shown between two broken lines throughout the book. As with most stage directions, feel free to interpret them in the light of your own situation.

SETTING THE SCENE
A QUICK DRINK IN THE BAR

Just before the show starts, a senior company executive meets his friend, a theatre producer, for a quick drink. Strain above the hubbub and clatter and you can hear them discussing the curious notion of using theatre techniques in business.

EXECUTIVE: This show better be good.

PRODUCER: Why particularly?

EXECUTIVE: I've had a lousy day at the office, I don't need a bad night out as well.

PRODUCER: Don't tell me, 'economy tight, competition closing in, impossible targets, can't get the staff, blood out of a stone', all the usual moans.

EXECUTIVE: Well it's a tough world.

PRODUCER: But why do all you business executives behave as if you've been singled out by the universe for a tough time?

EXECUTIVE: There's a lot of pressure out there, challenge, problems, grind...

PRODUCER: It's the same for everyone.

EXECUTIVE: Apart from you. You're dealing with glamour, magic and make believe.

PRODUCER: No, I'm dealing with deadlines, expectations, limited resources, underfunding and demanding standards.

EXECUTIVE: Look, I'm talking about the cut and thrust of commercial pressure in the corporate world, not flouncing around on stage.

PRODUCER: I do know about pressure. My people have to deliver outstanding performance night after night. No matter what the circumstances, the show has to go on. The difference is we know we can't be really successful if the whole process is misery, which is what it sounds like at your place.

EXECUTIVE: So you think we could have 'Les Mis' instead of misery and deliver commercial success at the same time?

PRODUCER: The creative industries in Britain generate over £100 billion a year. And Hollywood movie exports are worth more than the GDP of some small countries. Show business is big business. So if you want to stop having bad weeks at work, you might want to open your mind to the possibilities theatre can offer.

EXECUTIVE: Like what?

PRODUCER: Listen, what if our ideas could help you harness talent, motivate, build trust, promote creativity and innovation, produce exceptional performance and have some fun as well? Would you stop whingeing and get on board?

EXECUTIVE: What do you mean by exceptional performance?

PRODUCER: No cast of actors commits to producing a mediocre production of a play. They always want it to be exceptional, memorable, even ground breaking. 'Average' simply isn't an option. Instead, there's a relentless quest for the definitive production – for extraordinary, rather than ordinary, performance. Why do you go to the theatre or the cinema?

EXECUTIVE: I want a great time, I want to be blown away, I want to be thrilled.

PRODUCER: Exactly. Audiences are demanding.

EXECUTIVE: So are my customers. If I can't delight them, then others will.

PRODUCER: And the same goes for your staff. They want an exciting place to work. So, can I interest you in my ideas?

EXECUTIVE: OK, I'll listen, but if you start behaving like a luvvie then I'm out of here.

PRODUCER: Deal.

★ ★ ★ ★ ★

Mere metaphor?

Business people have always been smart enough to seek inspiration from other areas of activity, whether from the military, sport, cooking, sea life or even insect swarms.

'If you want to be successful – think theatre!' Charles Handy, social philosopher

Using theatre as a source for inspiring individual, team and organizational change is also hardly new. For over a decade we have used theatre techniques with our clients and have witnessed their impact on unlocking people's and companies' potential.

Theatre is more than a mere metaphor for business to play with. In fact, applying performing arts technology energizes, motivates and inspires people to give of their best – to become, in effect, star performers.

There is a growing awareness in many companies of the power of such techniques, which are moving from being a hidden source of expertise to becoming much more widely exploited. Here, for example, are just some of the ways companies use theatre-based processes to enhance business performance:

★ Role play has been a learning tool for many years. It is now common to see professional actors hired to play one side of a situation, in both development programmes and assessment situations. Many development initiatives, for instance, use Augustus Boal's 'forum theatre' in which audiences join in the drama and interactively change the course of events. Boal developed the concept of the 'theatre of the oppressed' when working with disenfranchised people in Latin America. It has become a useful approach in business, perhaps because so many staff feel similarly downtrodden.

★ Shakespeare's plays, such as *Henry V*, are regularly used to explore leadership.

★ Sometimes team-building exercises involve groups devising, directing and performing their own plays, which might reflect issues within their company.

★ Drama-based development sessions are being provided in all sorts of organizations to awaken, enliven and enrich people's working lives. And of course, few conferences would be complete without the theatricality of stage sets, lighting and dramatic music.

★ In *The Experience Economy*, Pine and Gilmore elaborate the theatrical idea in a thoughtful and businesslike way, applying it to customer service. They encourage the use of acting skills to create exciting experiences for clients, thus maximizing profits. Disney, for instance, has always used the theatre metaphor in order to 'put on a show' for the public. Out-front workers are called 'cast members' and they go 'on stage' to face the public. The personnel department is referred to as 'casting'.

★ Increasingly companies have to consider how they manage their talent. Given that the most talented 'star' performers can pick and choose their jobs, companies are having to behave more like the entertainment business in the way these people are managed.

★ The retail trade was an early exponent of using theatre to enhance performance and its offering to the public. From the beginning, natural cosmetics retailer The Body Shop saw a visit to its shops as a theatrical experience and ensured that its staff were equipped to make this happen. Supermarket chain Safeway has been training its store staff with theatre-based methods so that they can use their personality in interacting with customers.

★ Theatre is used to help in conflict resolution by showing all sides of a situation. A play is a great vehicle for illustrating different points of view, with each character having their say. The first step is getting characters to see the situation from another's point of view. There is also a healing and therapeutic process when a character's mask is stripped away and we see that behind it is a vulnerable human being with whom we may well be able to identify.

★ In the late 1960s schools realized the impact that drama-based methods could have. 'Theatre in education' allowed actors to take children through experiences simulating what it was like to, say, be evacuated in the Second World War, or work in a factory on a production line, or be discriminated against. Similar simulations are now used in the corporate world to enable managers to rehearse dealing with business problems.

★ The skill set studied by actors is similar to that needed by leaders in business, as we shall see later. Voice and movement experts coach people in enhancing their communication skills. Our own offering at MLA includes much of the above, but we have mainly specialized in putting the participant or client centre stage, using various acting techniques to improve work performance. These might cover areas such as presenting, improvising, understanding character, creativity, insight into leading and learning to coach.

Whether it is the elaborate make-up of Japanese Noh theatre or the masks of Greek drama, theatre of all kinds taps into a deep human need to witness magical change. The arts generally have always offered the promise of transformation, of realizing potential. Many of our great myths and legends include moments of great symbolic transformation.

Even traditional British pantomime stemmed from ancient stories involving a belief in magical change. Have you ever seen the delight on a child's face as they witness the transformation scene in which, for instance, Cinderella finally gets to go to the ball with her coach and horses? It's a useful reminder that our inner child still longs for such a possibility. In the right circumstances, people long for change rather than fearing it.

Every day in every organization, the curtain rises, the lights go on and the performance must begin. Many companies also have to create a transformation and bring about change. They face a similar challenge of creating a kind of magic that thrills customers, employees and shareholders alike.

TAKE YOUR SEATS PLEASE

A bell signals that it's time for the bar to close and for people to move to the auditorium. On the way, the company executive continues chatting to his producer friend.

EXECUTIVE: Since I saw you last I've been suffering from a bout of 'consultantitis'.

PRODUCER: I'm sorry to hear that.

EXECUTIVE: Yeah, we're doing a bit of downsizing, rightsizing, restructuring and process reengineering.

PRODUCER: Sounds painful. Any of your *people* involved in that sort of thing?

EXECUTIVE: We'll come to them later.

PRODUCER: Seems a bit back to front to me. Surely it starts with your people?

EXECUTIVE: Don't start talking all that touchy-feely stuff with me. I get enough of that from my HR director.

PRODUCER: It's just that I can't imagine myself trying to produce outstanding performance if I and my cast felt like cogs in a machine. I'd never get any of my performers to go for that.

EXECUTIVE: We have to get the systems straight.

PRODUCER: I'm sure you do, but can't your own people sort that out? I always start with individuals, because it's individuals who make the difference.

EXECUTIVE: That's certainly true. It's the only competitive advantage we've got.

PRODUCER: If I were looking at your company, instead of reorganizing everyone else, I'd start with you.

EXECUTIVE: Me?

PRODUCER: Yes. It has to start with you first, before looking at other people. Then I'd find out how people work together in teams, and lastly at the organization as a whole.

EXECUTIVE: That makes sense, I suppose, but you seem to be implying that I need to change in some way.

PRODUCER: I'm not sure, but I reckon if you could get your own act together, you'd know more about how to raise everyone else's performance.

★ ★ ★ ★ ★

THE LIGHTS DIM

You just have time to glance at the programme. In the theatre of change there are three key acts leading to exceptional performance:

'You must be the change you wish to see in the world.'
Mahatma Gandhi

★ Act I: Getting your *personal* act together.
★ Act II: Getting your *team's* act together.
★ Act III: Getting your *organization's* act together.

Focusing on these crucial elements of the drama is not our idiosyncratic view of what makes a real difference. They reflect a combination of the practical wisdom of successful business people, detailed research, the views of pioneering thinkers on transforming companies and our own experience of leading change. And one thing we know for sure: you can't transform anything unless you're

first willing to lead the way yourself. So that's where we'll start.
Curtain up – it's time to act.

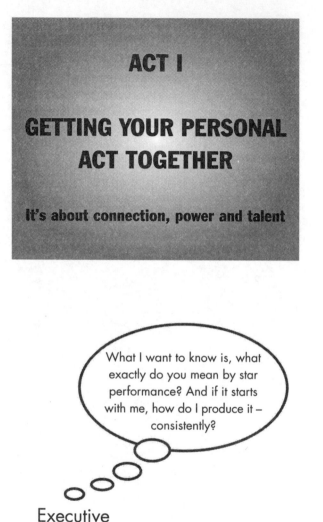

Executive

The curtain rises and lights up the three essential elements needed in order to transform personal performance:

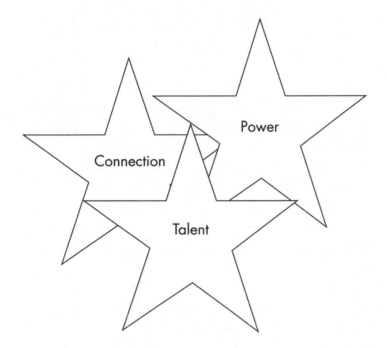

Act I is made up of the following three scenes:

★ Scene 1 – *Personal connection*: feeling closely aligned to the enterprise in some way.
★ Scene 2 – *Personal power*: taking control and responsibility for what's going on.
★ Scene 3 – *Personal talent*: having the appropriate skills.

SCENE 1
PERSONAL CONNECTION

It's appraisal time at a Midlands car parts plant. Dawn, a trusted and frustrated member of the credit control department, enters her line manager's office.

MANAGER: Sit yourself down, Dawn.

DAWN: Thanks.

MANAGER: You don't have to look so fed up.

DAWN: What do you expect? I hate appraisals. I try my best all year, then I come in here, you tell me my performance isn't up to scratch, I haven't hit the right competency level or something, and therefore I can't get any more money. Sorry, am I supposed to be smiling?

MANAGER: OK, fair enough. That's why we're changing things.

DAWN: Don't tell me, I get to appraise you, do I? That'll be the day.

MANAGER: You're not far off, actually.

Dawn pretends to fall off her chair in shock.

MANAGER: Listen, they're not even called appraisals any more. This is a performance and development review. (*Quickly, before Dawn can interrupt*) Before you tell me it makes no difference what it's called, there are other changes as well. The focus of this session is now about your development. Of course, we need to see how you've been performing and areas where it's difficult to deliver your goals, but my job is to support you in improving – and I doubt I'll do that simply by docking your wages.

DAWN: Have you been on a course or something?

MANAGER: No, it's just part of a bigger initiative where we're trying to see what it will take for each person in this company to deliver outstanding performance. And I don't reckon that the old appraisal system stands any chance of doing that, do you?

DAWN: It's a waste of time.

MANAGER: Everyone here is capable of delivering excellent performance and I want to find out what it will take to get that.

> DAWN: If you're serious and you really want me to do my best around here, then a few things need to change. Some in me, I admit. And some other things too…
>
> MANAGER: Well, let's sort it out together. I want to agree with you what needs to happen for you to perform at your best. Clearly you have some ideas and so do I. Come on, let's get cracking.

What does it take for Dawn – or any of us – to perform outstandingly? To do so, we need to feel a strong personal connection to the enterprise. How do you get such a connection?

Stars by the dozen queued up to be humiliated when comedy duo The Right Size performed their West End hit *The Play What I Wrote*, featuring a secret celebrity guest. There had to be something in it for the celebrity, other than a perverse desire to be made to look foolish in public or the parsimonious appearance fee on offer.

Or why would an actor with movie-star status, such as Ralph Fiennes, perform Shakespeare in an improvised auditorium in a derelict studio by the canal in London's rundown Shoreditch area? Similarly, something special must have persuaded Patrick Stewart, from *Star Trek* and *X-Men*, to revive a little-known J B Priestly play at the West Yorkshire Playhouse. These stars can pick and choose their work and go anywhere. When it comes to a choice between a multimillion-dollar pay packet from a blockbuster movie or the tiny fees from performing to a live audience, it has to be something other than the bottom line that makes them go for Shakespeare or Yorkshire rather than Minghella or Hollywood.

'Man cannot live by Bard alone.'
Donald Sinden, actor

What attracts them? It may be a particular part they want to play or a director they want to work with. There will be something exceptional about the enterprise that compels them to sign up and commit themselves to the production. We produce our best work when we have a personal investment in the enterprise. To perform outstandingly we need to feel connected to our work, aligned to the project in some way.

Of course there are actors, just as there are people in businesses, who do it only for the money. As Bob Hoskins explained when asked why he appeared in television commercials for British Telecom: 'I can give you 250,000 reasons why I agreed.'

Yet when it comes to creating star performance, research constantly confirms that money is definitely not everything. Surveys consistently reveal that while people need a certain basic financial reward, this seldom gets their juices flowing.

What really makes us feel connected to an enterprise normally involves the following questions:

★ What's in it for me?
★ Do I fit in?
★ Can I make an impact?
★ Does it *mean* anything?
★ Can I express myself?

There's got to be some sort of personal connection for us to give of our best. This can be because we feel we belong and know we can make an impact, or because the enterprise has meaning for us and aligns with our values and integrity. Ultimately, we need to feel that we can express ourselves in the role we are performing.

Feel you belong

Part of connection involves a definite sense of belonging. Ask actors in a successful production what they like most about it and the answer is often 'the privilege of working with talented colleagues'.

While making the film *Mrs Brown* about Queen Victoria, Scottish comedian and actor Billy Connolly, who played man-

'Whatever I get paid, it doesn't make me a better actor. It doesn't make me work harder. I arrive on time to work just as I did when I got paid scale.'
Julia Roberts, actor

'It's really why I do this job. Not for performances – not for plays – not for money – but for the satisfaction of having a really good rehearsal where the excitement of discovery spreads from actor to actor.'
Peter Hall, director

PERSONAL BENEFITS

Start by asking yourself:

★ Why am I doing what I'm doing?
★ What's in it for me?
★ What are the benefits of success?
★ What do I personally get out of the process?
★ Will I advance my career or reputation in some way if I am successful?
★ Could I maintain my desired lifestyle without this current job or career?
★ If I won the Lottery, would I still be doing this job?
★ Do I have a passion for the work I do?
★ What must I do to be totally committed to its success?

servant John Brown, raved about the work of his co-star Judi Dench as Queen Victoria. He was amazed that she could repeat a scene a dozen times, always with renewed passion. Independently, Dench said how marvellous Connolly was and what a joy it was to work with him. As another example, Whoopi Goldberg commented how acting with Maggie Smith in *Sister Act* pushed her to produce her best work, out of respect and admiration for such a great actor. The members of an acting company want to feel that they are aligned and therefore able to admire each other's work.

It's no fun acting in a play if you think everyone else is performing badly. And if everyone thinks that, the show certainly faces a crisis of confidence. It's exactly the same on the corporate stage. When you look around and see people in roles for which they are clearly suited, it builds confidence and trust in those leading the enterprise. But nothing is more demoralizing than doing our best, only to be let down because others don't have the necessary skills or the right attitude. We want to work with like-minded people

> 'I would have paid to be in the production, because of the people involved.'
> Kate Winslett, actor, about the film *Iris*

who share similar values. And even if they aren't literally like-minded, sharing our ideas and opinions, we want them to be like-*hearted*, so we feel a connection with them.

This is not an excuse for employing clones. Teams need diversity, a rich cultural mix that offers different points of view. It is pointless seeking to achieve 'fit' by simply bringing in similar people. They may share our values, but they need to offer a wide range of alternative skills and come from diverse backgrounds.

If the power rests with the talent, then every individual needs to feel that they belong. When people believe that, they take ownership of all kinds of problems and tasks, often without prompting. It is 'their' company and they assume that if an issue comes their way, they own it and do something about. This makes it easy to know when things aren't right.

'If you have a "yes-man" working for you, one of you is redundant.'
Barry Rand, Xerox

Make an impact

Being connected means knowing that your contribution, no matter how small, is important. Alec Guinness referred to the joy he got from some of the smallest, sometimes unnamed, parts in Shakespeare and the opportunities they offered. Actors refer to tiny roles like these as 'a cough and a spit'. They have to face the issue of whether they are really making much of a contribution to the production as a whole.

In the 1970s the UK's National Theatre experimented with creating an ensemble acting company. It asked the star performers to accept small parts in some productions, as well as leading ones in others. Laurence Olivier modelled the way by playing the butler Plucheux in Feydeau's *A Flea in Her Ear*. He never saw his role as insignificant, however, instead milking it for all it was worth. He often won a round of applause on his exits, confirming the adage that 'there are no small parts, only small actors'.

And in business we only perform well when we know that no amount of goals, quality standards or indicators of performance replace a basic grasp of 'why what I do matters'. On a practical level this means do you have a say, is there freedom to make some decisions, do you hold any budgets, are you invited to contribute, are your ideas and suggestions duly rewarded?

If you play the corporate equivalent of a walk-on part, how do you make an impact? Hierarchies, committees, control systems, rigid procedures, unstated 'rules', even teamworking can all conspire to stop us making a difference. And it is a two-way process. For everyone's contribution to be heard, everyone's performance needs to be visible. Dramatic success can only truly be achieved if we have the potential to make an impact. If you cannot do that at the moment, it is time to explore your avenues of influence. But first, be very clear what you are trying to achieve and what that means to you.

Clarify your personal purpose

Every day we meet people who are hungry for something more in their work. It is impossible to see how organizations consisting of cynical time-servers, who are sitting around waiting for retirement

PERSONAL IMPACT

Try an impact audit:

★   Do I make a difference?
★   How does my job contribute to the whole?
★   Does what I do help the organization succeed?
★   If I didn't come in tomorrow, what would be missed?
★   Do I have the power to influence decisions?
★   Could I make something happen if I wanted to?

> 'Human beings want to love their organizations – they don't want to work for a set of bastards. People seek meaning in their work and will start to creep out the door if they find none.'
> Jim McNeish, Kingfisher Group

or redundancy packages, can ever attain exceptional performance. Something has to shift for them to stand a chance. One element of this is whether their work provides a sense of purpose. What is the point for you?

Jim McNeish, executive development director for Kingfisher Group, says: 'The view that companies have a simple agenda of making money for shareholders is waning. People are becoming more aware of the larger purpose of organizations.'

When you spend time reflecting on issues such as:

★ Why am I here?
★ What does success look and feel like?
★ What really matters to me?
★ Does my work express my passion?
★ Am I doing the work I want to do?
★ Am I living the life I want to live?

you are exploring questions that are just as significant and vital to personal success as the more traditional one: What does the bottom line say this quarter?

Making sure that you feel connected to your organization is not so much a science, more a matter of being 'in tune' with the culture. We feel comfortable with what's going on. This means using creative ways to connect us with each other and with corporate goals. This is clearly a messy area with few simple solutions, but having an exciting vision, knowing where you are going as an organization, sharing values, delighting customers and feeling that you make a contribution are all important elements in the process.

Actors benefit from knowing what roles they hunger to play, what medium they want to work in, how they want their audiences to feel as a result of their performances. Do they want to see their name up in lights, for instance, or in the cast of a soap opera, in a theatre programme, on billboards, in community theatre, as part of an ensemble company or at the Academy awards?

> 'This is the true joy of life – being used for a purpose recognized by yourself as a mighty one.'
> George Bernard Shaw, playwright

Anthony Sher's first job as an actor was at the Liverpool Everyman theatre. One evening he was having a drink with his director, Alan Dosser.

ALAN DOSSER: What do you want to say as an actor?

ANTHONY SHER: I don't 'say' anything, I'm an actor. Acting is interpretive, not creative. It's directors and writers who have anything to 'say'.

ALAN DOSSER: Bollocks! You won't become a really good actor until you've put yourself on the line, until the job's vital. What plays you do, why you do them, how you do them; it's got to mean something to you before it's going to mean anything to the audience.

Dosser inspired the young actor to think differently and it was a turning point in his life. Sher went on to 'say' quite a lot. He has not only played the major Shakespearean roles, but also starred in films and on television and published four books. Would he have made such an impression without the inspiration of a director like Alan Dosser, who got him to think about the meaning of his work? Probably not. It is essential for all of us to challenge ourselves with these sorts of questions.

INCIDENTS WITH MEANING

Allowing company members to share examples of meaningful action can be an excellent reminder for people and help revitalize them. You could use a team meeting or an awayday to ask yourself and your colleagues the question: What's an example of something that happens in the company that gives you meaning in your work or expresses a sense of purpose? What kind of incident epitomizes this?

Such success stories can help people reconnect with their purpose. This is why mission and vision statements can sometimes be simply glorified goals, rather than expressions of purpose that have genuine meaning for people. The real question is: How am I acting in my everyday drama that makes me proud to be involved? (There is more on this in Act II, Scene 3.)

Where do you want to see your name writ large? There are always choices we have to make about the direction our life is going in and it helps to take some time to reflect on our preferences. Personal statements of purpose help us monitor our commitment to the organization for which we work and whether it meets our needs for meaning.

Live your values

Having strong personal values and feeling these are aligned to the organization helps you commit to the enterprise and perform at your best. That is why we are likely to choose to work for people with integrity. Integrity now means moral soundness and probity, yet the word comes from wholeness and completeness, describing a person who has integrated their values and their actions. The best actors certainly want to work for directors who have it. Only when they sense this in a director will they feel safe enough to take the kind of risks in rehearsal that make brilliance possible.

PURPOSE STATEMENT

There are ways in which you can clarify a personal statement for yourself. In development exercises with participants on workshops, we help people become aware of:

a   Their unique qualities or skills.
b   How they express these qualities or talents.
c   The effect they want to create in the workplace.

These in turn create a personal purpose statement such as:

My purpose is that I will use my (a) (unique qualities) _____
through/in/as (b) (role/activity) ————————————————— in order that/to (c) (intention)
_____

Who you are and what you stand for govern how you work and what you can hope to achieve. Julia Middleton, who started the hugely successful charity Common Purpose, believes that it was her rebellious streak that drove her success. Ben Cohen and Jerry Greenfield, the rebels who founded Ben & Jerry's, were driven by their love of ice cream and desire to produce a 'home-style' product. Ricardo Semler, president of Brazilian manufacturer Semco, was driven by his anti-authoritarian values. Early on he decided he didn't want to spend his life as a manager controlling other people. He would much rather do something more creative and entrust people to their own self-control. Anita Roddick, always seeking alternative ways of spreading her Body Shop brand, often looked at which way the cosmetic industry was going and deliberately went in the opposite direction.

If you have strong personal values and integrity, you tend to stand out from the crowd. You are unafraid to speak up for

'Integrate what you believe in, in every single area of your life.'
Meryl Streep, actor

The board members of an organization are doing a 'values exercise'. Each is writing what they personally value about the company on Post-it™ notes and sticking them on a board. In another area they are also listing what they definitely don't value. Soon they have covered all the areas with a mass of multicoloured notes. They stand back, reflect and begin clustering the pieces of paper together. There is a mass of notes with 'honesty' written on them, and another cluster with 'quality'. 'Professionalism' features strongly, as do 'teamworking', 'customers' and 'intelligence'.

In the negative area there are 'money grabbing', 'lying', 'expediency' and assorted other activities that they spurn.

After a while, a senior partner studies the positive values on the board and quietly says: 'All I know is, I want to work in a firm that lives out these values. If I really felt my working day was about this, I'd retire a fulfilled human being.'

'Whether you're an artist, an actor, a writer, in business, or whatever you do, you should have a barometer of what's truthful and what isn't truthful in your work. You have to be able to look at your own work like you're looking at your toughest competitor's work.'
Dustin Hoffman, actor

yourself and what you believe in and you gain respect for doing so. As Julia Middleton says, her background encouraged her to 'say boo to a goose' and not to be terrified of anyone. While there is a fine line between having opinions and being opinionated, you need to be willing to take a stand, have a point of view and bring your personal experience to bear on issues that are important.

Integrity applies to work–life balance as well. The managers who seem to suffer the most stress are those who live a kind of double life. They reserve their compassion and humour for their social life, while maintaining a hard-nosed ruthlessness in the workplace. The most effective business performers don't compartmentalize in this way. Instead, they bring their whole persona to the organization.

Getting your personal act together normally means ensuring that you work for an organization that has integrity and inspiring values. It's not enough that these values simply look good on plaques on the wall or mouse mats. They need to be practised and embodied by your colleagues. They have meaning because they are

VALUES GAP

There are many ways to explore the chasm between espoused values and actual ones within your organization. Try using the image of the Shakespearean fool or court jester, who debunks pomposity. Ask a colleague to sit on a 'throne' and formally pronounce the organization's values. From behind them up pops the fool, who enjoys 'telling it like it is', proclaiming the truth as they experience it from an individual viewpoint. For example:

KING: We really value people here.
FOOL: Which is why we have just got rid of several hundred!
KING: We're committed to giving outstanding service.
FOOL: So long as it doesn't affect our quarterly returns!
KING: We believe in open communication.
FOOL: On an openly 'need to know' basis.

After the jesting there needs to be an informed discussion about why such gaps exist and what might be done about them. This dramatic way of exploring the issue tends to provoke incisive action.

acted on. And if your company is lacking in this way, then you have some work to do!

Identify your individual star quality

To be connected to an enterprise, you need to feel you can express yourself. But what is the 'self' in question? This demands an ability to know ourselves and what is special and distinctive about us.

Every agent or casting director seeks clarity about what a particular actor is offering. It is no good wanting to look like Jude Law or have the vocal dexterity of Anthony Hopkins, the comic timing of Felicity Kendall, or the physical pliability of Jim Carey – if you don't. Actors have to face the brutal facts and know their strengths and limitations.

In his research and conclusions about what makes companies great, Jim Collins revealed a common tendency to ensure that they 'first got the right people on the bus, and the wrong people off the bus, and the right people in the right seats'. In other words, outstanding performance depends first on who you cast and their capabilities.

Business, like theatre, is hungry for stars. By 'stars' we mean the enduring ones who continuously produce outstanding performance, are talented, and have a clear sense of identity, with a distinctive 'voice'. We certainly do not mean the 'famous-for-fifteen minutes' celebrities, who mainly rely on glamour or notoriety. The kind of stars who are worthwhile are those who are defiantly themselves, expressing their own values, beliefs, knowledge and integrity and who therefore make a unique and invaluable contribution.

Corporations may want star performers, yet they face two separate challenges in casting the right talent for the job. First, it can be a struggle for anyone to be fully themselves because since childhood we have been expected to conform and become like other people.

Secondly, companies can be ruthless machines for enforcing conformity. Personal success can depend on being highly adaptable to corporate norms. Consequently, we often sacrifice our distinctive qualities. Instead, we learn to adapt and wear a mask, sometimes forgetting that we are doing so.

For example, the much used 'competency framework' is a way of enforcing conformity to usually narrow definitions of what constitutes desired leadership qualities. While such a framework may be valuable in helping us organize development, it can be very restricting. Had they faced such demands to fit in, would we have ever heard of Danny De Vito, Mo Mowlem, Eddie Izzard, Oprah Winfrey, Stephen Hawking, Victoria Wood, Stelios Haji-Ioannou,

> 'God makes stars. It's up to the producers to find them.'
> Sam Goldwyn,
> film producer

> 'Your value as an actor is how different you are from everybody else, not how similar.'
> Donald Sinden, actor

CASTABILITY

When theatrical agents or casting directors interview an actor, they are always looking for what's distinctive. The actors' directory *Spotlight* even puts them in categories, such as 'younger character actor' or 'leading actor'. Performers need to know how they are seen by others if they are to maximize their employability. They need to be aware of their style.

'How do you see my particular style?' can be a sobering question to pursue. The words people use and the images they evoke all convey your leadership style and whether it is a source of inspiration. Why not go out and seek this sort of feedback?

Actors get continual feedback from colleagues, directors, audiences, critics, agents and casting directors. That is why 360 degree feedback is becoming so valuable in companies. It gives you a rounded view of yourself as others see you.

By the way, here's another potentially revealing exercise you can try: Putting vanity or wish fulfilment aside, which actor or actress would you cast to be you in a play or film about your life? Why? What is it about them that you like, that makes you want them to be you?

Madonna, Michael Dell, Kathy Burke, Ted Turner, Penelope Keith or Frank McCourt? They dared to be different and it is their individuality that helped them triumph.

A highly successful operations director of a well-known UK company was being groomed to become managing director. He was told discreetly that he needed to stop being so ready to say what he thought. Also, to satisfy City conventions, he was urged to start wearing suits. Said a close colleague with sadness: 'I see him slowly becoming a grey person. It's like I'm watching one arm turning grey while the rest remains special. Soon, though, maybe the rest will follow.'

'One of the beauties of having a career as an actor is the old cliché: you are your instrument. You go through life and what you go through becomes a part of the work you do. And, if it's not too early in the morning, I always come to it with relish.'
Ian McShane, actor

Expand your range

Expressing your distinctive self doesn't mean that you don't have scope to widen your capabilities. Orson Welles once gave a one-man show of Shakespearean readings in Phoenix, Arizona, and found only five people in the audience. 'Allow me to introduce myself,' he began. 'I am an actor, a writer, a stage director of both films and plays, an architect, a painter, a brilliant cook, an expert on the Corrida, a conjuror, a collector, a connoisseur, an enfant terrible and an authority on modern art. How come there are so many of *me* and so few of you?' Then he walked off.

While Welles was an exceptionally talented and complex human being, there is a curious paradox about individual star performance. On one hand, the best performers are always themselves; they do not try to be someone else or slavishly imitate others. On the other, individuals excel when they are highly adaptable, drawing on all parts of themselves, using the 'whole person'.

Mature actors know that within themselves they have accumulated a vast array of characters, which they can then portray externally. This internal cast of characters expresses different psychological aspects. And it is not only actors who possess this rich inner theatre; we all do. Some psychologists refer to them as subpersonalities, but we see them rather as *dramatis personae*.

Dealing with different work situations requires us to call on new aspects of ourselves. Understanding our inner resources in this way gives us a larger repertoire and more options, should the plot of our everyday drama require them.

For us to perform at our best we need to be able to access this rich inner resource in an authentic way. It is a common fallacy that acting is all about pretence, fooling an audience by pretending to be another person. That is mainly a sign of *bad* acting. Such per-

'Every character I've ever played is me, because there are about 40 people inside me and I just take away 39 of them for any particular role.'
Angelina Jolie, actor

formances usually fail to move the audience emotionally, because we remain aware that something is not right.

We are only convinced when actors use a truthful part of themselves to portray a character. Someone playing an angry person must find an inner source of anger. Playing a grieving role, the actor discovers and expresses some existing sadness within. Much of the 'method' school of acting, made famous by actors such as Marlon Brando, Gina Rowlands and Al Pacino, focuses on using a 'sense memory' to generate genuine emotion in a character.

To help you reach for star performance, consider your inner cast of characters (see overleaf). Look inside at what different aspects of yourself you could potentially draw on to be more effective at work or to handle a particular situation. When you fully access your inner cast, you begin to become more effective and are able to bring a wider range of personal resources to deal with ever-changing challenges.

> 'Acting is revelation, not imitation. Actors in performance reveal their inner lives.'
> Peter Hall, director

Reach for star performance

Finally, you can only achieve great performance if you have personal standards that define such excellence. Even then, its achievement can remain somewhat of a mystery. After a particularly stunning performance as Othello, Laurence Olivier was discovered in a state of near despair. Asked why he was so low after such a wonderful delivery, he snapped, 'Yes, I know it was good, but I just don't know how I did it.'

Some performers describe extraordinary experiences like this as being 'in the zone'. 'When I'm in the zone, I feel freer, less in control, more susceptible,' says Meryl Streep. However, she goes on to describe the difficulty of replicating such outstanding performance: 'I wish I had a codified method, but I don't have. I'm nearly 50 and each job comes along and I don't know how I'm going to approach it.'

INNER CAST OF CHARACTERS

What about your own inner bureaucrat, inner lover, inner enthusiast, inner controller, inner beach bum, inner visionary or whatever? In identifying some of your inner characters in this way and getting to know them better, you might be able to expand your range of leadership. Being able to call on these different aspects of yourself to meet different situations enhances your effectiveness. So, having identified your characters, explore:

★   When does this character seem to take over?
★   What seems to trigger this character's appearance?
★   What control do I have over this character?
★   What influence does this character have on my leadership?
★   Does the character get in the way or instead really help?
★ ⸱ How does this character communicate?

The issue even for experienced performers is how to maximize the chances of repeating excellence consistently, so that it is no mere fluke. As the saying goes: 'Everyone has butterflies, it's the professional who gets them to fly in formation.'

In reaching for the stars, we need to understand that peak performance is just that, a special occurrence that is not easily explainable or instantly repeatable. Striving for it allows us to achieve excellence more consistently.

So how can we apply this to business, where such dramatic performance is increasingly necessary? For some people peak performance emerges spontaneously, without any support from external factors. But more often than not, it will be the result of the 'connecting' factors described in this scene, plus a couple of other crucial elements. The first of these is personal power.

PEAK EXPERIENCES

Actress Stephanie Cole, best known for her television performances in *Talking Heads*, *Tenko* and *Waiting for God*, identifies four key ingredients for producing an exceptional performance.

'The first is having done your homework so you absolutely feel that you can inhabit the character you play. You are at one with the part. Secondly, there's a feeling resembling an inward-focused mass of contained energy. Thirdly, confidence, that the internal critic is minimized.' She quotes Hegel, who described this as 'getting rid of the watchman at the gates of creativity'. 'And the final ingredient is relaxation. Letting go and allowing it to happen.'

Stephanie explains that 'of course, you can't force any of this to happen; you can only recognize it when it does, and be grateful'.

We have researched this extensively with many performers and similar elements keep arising. Here is how various professional actors we have interviewed describe what produces these peak experiences:

★ Prepare, prepare, prepare – then throw away the preparation, trust risk and surrender.
★ The dynamic between structure and freedom creates some magic.
★ I have a heightened sense of well-being.
★ I feel I am safe in a dangerous place.
★ Wanting to tell my character's story.
★ Trusting the director and their vision – the sense of a safe playpen where creativity can flourish and anything becomes possible.
★ A feeling of unity and union with my fellow actors and the audience.
★ Train hard, work, practice, practice – get depressed – more practice – despair – more practice – terror of performing live – let go.
★ Leave my body – let my instinct have full reign and get out and *stay* out of the way.

To anyone seeking the elusive answer to the challenge of generating outstanding performance, it certainly seems to be a mix of structure, discipline, hard work and focus, and then having the confidence to let go and fly.

SCENE 2
PERSONAL POWER

During the scene change, a whispered conversation takes place.

EXECUTIVE: I wish my people would take more initiative. They seem to think that
    if they keep their heads down, we'll somehow be successful.

PRODUCER: You can't do that in the theatre, of course.

EXECUTIVE: How so?

PRODUCER: There's no place to hide, is there? An actor's performance is so
    visible – they present their product directly to their customers. If it goes
    well they get rapturous applause, but if it goes wrong they experience
    painful humiliation. I tell you, such visibility is sobering.

EXECUTIVE: I could do with my people feeling 'on the spot' like that.

PRODUCER: It starts with delegating responsibility. There's nothing I or the director
    can do once the show is on the road. It's over to the actors and the crew.
    They have the power to make choices – and then celebrate their successes.

EXECUTIVE: If I give my lot freedom to make decisions, I want them to be accountable.

PRODUCER: Power and responsibility go hand in hand. I think if you give
    people responsibility and then make their performance visible, by
    highlighting their contribution maybe you'll get what you want.

EXECUTIVE: Talking of which, the lights are coming on again…

★ ★ ★ ★ ★

Be a chooser, not a victim

There is a direct link between how effective you are at work and
how much responsibility you take on. The more proactive you are,
the more likely you are to make things happen and be successful.
This goes to the heart of how you approach your entire working life
and, more generally, how companies can seek to unlock people's
potential so they can perform outstandingly.

The reverse is also true: the less you take responsibility for yourself and your contribution, the harder you will find it to be effective. The relationship between responsibility and effectiveness looks like this:

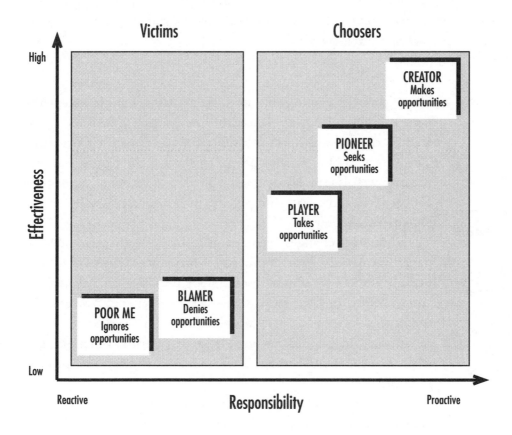

Responsibility comes from your ability to respond. You may not be able to control the conditions around you, but you can choose how to respond to them. People become star performers because they take increasing responsibility for ever-widening areas of their lives.

TEAM MEMBER: (*Arriving rushed, hot and bothered*) Sorry I'm late for the meeting. It wasn't my fault. It was the impossible queue in the canteen. I was stuck there for ever. There were far too many people. It's ridiculous.

COLLEAGUE: But you were one of those who created the log-jam, weren't you?

TEAM MEMBER: You're right. (*Goes out and comes in again, walking tall*) I apologize for being late. I was partly responsible. I helped make an enormous queue for lunch in the canteen. What an achievement!

In the comic example above nothing actually changes except the person's sense of power. Instead of being a victim to the circumstances, they take ownership and playfully reframe their situation. This sort of approach helps people embrace change positively and perform well. As the saying goes: 'You are not responsible for your background and circumstances, but you are responsible for the person you become.'

Many big changes in companies look perfectly reasonable on paper, yet never deliver improved performance. Why? Often it is because leaders simply impose a major initiative on a workforce and therefore the clear message they are conveying is: 'You're a victim of this decision.' People consequently feel powerless and often resentful. Why should anyone strive to perform outstandingly when in a moment they can be reorganized, restructured or even removed?

Victims not only resist taking responsibility, they blame other people, find comfort in being reactive rather than proactive, and spend time moaning and demotivating those around them. By contrast, *choosers* are proactive, continually seeking to improve, have a 'can do' attitude, and take responsibility for themselves and for making things happen.

'A play needs to be discovered, uncovered, one might almost say liberated. Every single actor has a personal responsibility in this matter. Every scene, every part, needs to be implied from the bare text.

This is an active undertaking, not a passive one.'
Simon Callow, actor

To illustrate the notion of victims and choosers, here are two different responses to the same event.

Facts:
★ Jo has a boss called Ranjit.
★ Ranjit manages the department and is responsible to his superiors and to the department team.
★ Ranjit has asked Jo to produce a report on potential improvements to the department.
★ Jo has heard via a friend that several ideas from the report have already begun to be implemented.
★ Ranjit's superior, Kay, is apparently pleased at the changes being made.
★ The report itself has not yet been discussed with Jo.
★ Ranjit has not acknowledged receipt of the report to Jo.
★ Jo is currently awaiting news of a salary increase.

Jo's victim reaction:

I go to all that trouble to get my report in early and nobody cares. How dare Ranjit steal my ideas? It's outrageous that my ideas are being implemented without me being involved.

He hasn't even discussed it with me. Kay probably doesn't even know I exist. I only get to hear of anything through the grapevine. Ranjit's standing in my way and I'll never get more money. Well, I'm not going to help with any of the changes. It's typical of this company, Ranjit sucking up to Kay. People are always exploiting me and taking me for granted. Still, there's nothing I can do. What's the point?

Jo's chooser reaction:

Delivering the report early has really paid off: some of my suggestions are happening already. Even though Ranjit is incredibly busy, he has still found time to push ahead with my report. It was worth me spending time getting the ideas right because they're actually happening. I'll let Ranjit know how delighted I am things are moving. Mind you, I'm angry that Ranjit hasn't acknowledged getting the report and hasn't talked to me about it. I'm going to ask for a meeting with him. I'll mention that, despite the pressure he's under, I'd have liked to have been told first. And I'll look for an opportunity to ask if there's an update on my salary review.

Note: It's not about positive thinking and ignoring the problems. It's about taking responsibility and not being a victim to the situation. Nothing has changed in the circumstances, only in Jo's ability to respond.

There tend to be two sorts of victims:

★ The *poor mes*: so busy sulking and feeling sorry for themselves and enlisting sympathy that they ignore their opportunities.
★ The *blamers*: deny that there are any opportunities coming their way and would rather point at everything that is going wrong around them.

Development consultant Ian Moore, who previously worked on change issues at Norwich Union, suggested a further position in this spectrum of responsibility, namely the role of *spectator*, who merely observes opportunities and never commits. Such people often appear reasonable yet remain uninvolved fence-sitters – not great contributors to exceptional performance. As Elizabethan playwright Francis Bacon warned: 'In this theatre of man's life, it is reserved only for God and Angels to be lookers-on.'

There are several kinds of choosers. The *player* takes opportunities when they come along. This is hardly proactive, but is at least open to possibilities. An even more effective chooser is the *pioneer*, who seeks opportunities believing that whatever they do can make a difference. The pioneer is also willing to see the bigger picture. And, finally, there are entrepreneurs who make opportunities. These are the *creators*, people who take responsibility for making something out of nothing.

What they think and say

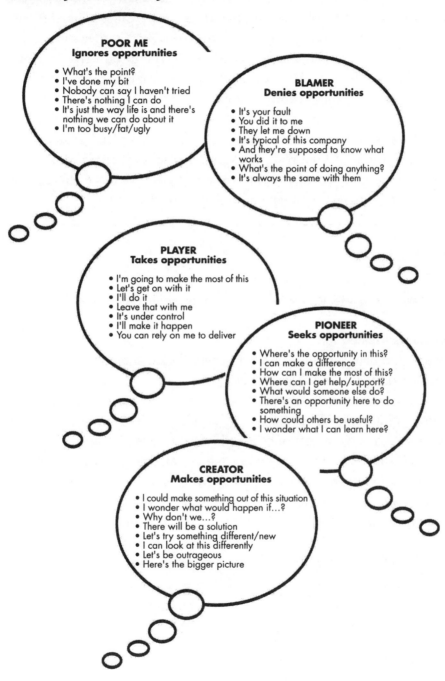

POOR ME
Ignores opportunities

- What's the point?
- I've done my bit
- Nobody can say I haven't tried
- There's nothing I can do
- It's just the way life is and there's nothing we can do about it
- I'm too busy/fat/ugly

BLAMER
Denies opportunities

- It's your fault
- You did it to me
- They let me down
- It's typical of this company
- And they're supposed to know what works
- What's the point of doing anything?
- It's always the same with them

PLAYER
Takes opportunities

- I'm going to make the most of this
- Let's get on with it
- I'll do it
- Leave that with me
- It's under control
- I'll make it happen
- You can rely on me to deliver

PIONEER
Seeks opportunities

- Where's the opportunity in this?
- I can make a difference
- How can I make the most of this?
- Where can I get help/support?
- What would someone else do?
- There's an opportunity here to do something
- How could others be useful?
- I wonder what I can learn here?

CREATOR
Makes opportunities

- I could make something out of this situation
- I wonder what would happen if…?
- Why don't we…?
- There will be a solution
- Let's try something different/new
- I can look at this differently
- Let's be outrageous
- Here's the bigger picture

Like most people, actors do their fair share of whingeing and moaning. Their pet hate is often their agent, who is blamed for not getting them enough opportunities for work. Yet they soon realize that venting their spleen on their agent is unproductive. It is only when they start taking responsibility for their own careers that they really make opportunities happen.

If you work with victims you soon know it from both their words and their deeds. Managers often complain about victim behaviour without really knowing what to do about it. Making the connection between responsibility and effectiveness opens up possible strategies for changing victims into choosers.

'Changing your agent is like changing deck-chairs on the *Titanic*.'
Actors' saying

VICTIMS INTO CHOOSERS

In workshops people suggest the following solutions for dealing with victim behaviour:

★ Make sure the person is listened to.
★ Show them the victim and chooser chart and ask where they are on it.
★ Treat them as choosers and you help them to become so.
★ Make sure they're clear about the standards of behaviour expected of them.
★ Operate zero tolerance for victim behaviour.
★ Apply peer pressure so that they understand the effect they have on others.
★ Get them to do a cost–benefit analysis: recognize the benefits they currently get from being victims, but look at the downside and show them the opportunities that are available should they opt to be choosers.
★ Make sure they know it's their victim behaviour that's unacceptable rather than who they are.
★ If all else fails, get rid of them, because the behaviour lets everyone else down.

OPPORTUNITY CARDS

Working with graduates at the London Stock Exchange some years ago, we came face to face with classic victim behaviour. The new graduates constantly complained about how powerless they were to affect anything in the Exchange. To encourage more 'creator' action we invented a way to explore this behaviour called 'opportunity cards'.

We have since used these in a variety of other companies and even hard-bitten managers seem to enjoy creating them. They are rather like 'Chance' cards in Monopoly, except that each contains a personal development challenge or task. Some cards are work related, e.g. 'Interview a senior manager and report back to the group about the company vision.' Or they may be a personal challenge, e.g. 'Persuade two colleagues to donate blood with you, and write a piece for the company magazine about the experience.' We create a pack of cards with perhaps 40 options and each person randomly picks a card.

The real measure of a person is not whether they complete the task but whether they turn it into a personal or company opportunity in some way. Participants have great success when they take the challenge purely as a starting point and create added value from it. Some have raised huge sums of money for charity, others have made recommendations that affected company policy and effectiveness.

Transforming victim attitudes and behaviour into chooser ones is an essential starting point for any change initiative or attempt to improve one's own or other people's performance. Under-performance will continue until the individual becomes the source of their own power, learning, development and success.

It may be hard to move ourselves and others from being, say, players or pioneers to becoming creators. Many of us may remain stuck in one of the earlier positions because of the circumstances that put us there. Some who appear victims in the work setting may still be high achievers outside it. Nevertheless, victim behaviour is

'Everyone is empowered to be creative and knowledgeable.'
James Dyson, manufacturer

like a black hole sucking in other people's energy and commitment and it has no place if we want to perform outstandingly.

Using your personal power effectively means being proactive. That starts with simply participating: getting involved and being willing to take responsibility. You may not yet be able to create opportunities, but you can start by seizing them when they come along.

Get empowered

Stage directors know that simply instructing actors how to perform seldom works. Come the performance, actors can always 'get their own back'. So while the director may have a firm idea of how the parts should be played, it is the actors who have the talent to deliver them. Rehearsal is all about allowing freedom to explore so that they can arrive at a personal interpretation.

'Empowerment' has become yet another piece of corporate speak, used so loosely as to forfeit its original meaning. What it really means is that people perform better when they have a sense of their own power.

Companies require their people to behave like grown-ups, yet continue to treat them like children. They control their behaviour,

---

POWER AUDIT

Try conducting an audit of the level of empowerment that exists where you work. What can and can't you do? Do you have freedom to make decisions, authorize expenditure or deal with situations?

If you feel restricted, then why not negotiate more control? Research shows that the people who are most happy in their work are the ones who feel they can exercise power and, to some extent, can control their own destiny.

---

they dictate what they can and can't do, and still they preach empowerment. They insist on a certain appearance, clothing, behaviour, time keeping and all sorts of restrictions. We even heard recently of a company where there was a thick book full of rules applying to 'dress-down Fridays'.

The big breakthrough for Ricardo Semler at his pioneering organization Semco in Brazil was to trust people as if they were adult human beings capable of making responsible decisions. Semler's approach allowed staff to set their own working times and job descriptions. Similarly, an employee of Hewlett-Packard told us that he felt free to work when he wanted and wear what he wanted. He knew that the company would trust him to deliver the level of performance that was necessary. He wasn't constrained by a 'tick box' approach to performance management (more on this in Act III, Scene 3). For you to perform outstandingly, you will probably need to feel that you have control of yourself, and to some extent of your work life as well.

> 'Once actors begin to think that working is doing the director a favour, they are finished.'
> Peter Brook, director

★ ★ ★ ★ ★

During the scene change:

EXECUTIVE: You can't give people empowerment, they have to take it and prove they're capable of using it.

PRODUCER: I agree. Ordering people to be empowered is a contradiction in terms. A bit like 'corporate intelligence'!

EXECUTIVE: Are you being sarcastic?

PRODUCER: Not me! People do need to feel invited. I've seen lots of businesses where people are so tightly controlled there's no way they feel encouraged to take real responsibility.

EXECUTIVE: I suppose I could start exploring this with my people, to see how they feel, what they want and what they could handle.

SCENE 3
PERSONAL TALENT

Star performance demands the raw material. You clearly need to develop the necessary skills and capabilities in the first place. But what are they? What do you personally need to produce dramatic success at work?

In the curriculum of the major drama schools, you find that the future stars of the performing arts must learn the following disciplines:

Voice	Body awareness	Flexibility/adaptability
Energy management	Relaxation	Emotional expression
Focus	Concentration	Sensory awareness
Memory	Listening	Understanding character
Improvising	Learning from mistakes	Giving/receiving feedback
Rhythm/timing	Being in the present moment	Pacing
Teamwork	Spontaneity	Risk taking
Creativity	Breathing	Eye contact
Communication	Interpretation	Establishing trust
Empathy	Discipline	Openness

Professional training usually lasts three years and then the actor goes out and auditions, hopefully on the road to stardom; or maybe not. A surprising number persist against apparently insurmountable odds. The continual striving for work and managing as a freelance demand yet more skills, including:

Resilience	Handling rejection and insecurity	Maintaining self-belief
Self-management	Promotion and marketing	A sense of humour

Yet what value has drama school training to a corporate leader?

Listen, I have no desire to stand on stage play-acting — what's all this got to do with me?

To produce outstanding results, wherever you are these days, people need just these sorts of talents

EXECUTIVE

PRODUCER

These and many more talents are, of course, also needed by managers in the workplace. Not so that they can become actors — there are more than enough of those already! While ordinary managers don't have to interpret a script, play a character or perform on a stage, they do require key elements of the actor's main skill set. These include energy management, the ability to express feelings, a sense of humour, focus, the ability to communicate clearly and an understanding of character.

Harness your energy

Great performers have vitality. They are vital in both senses of the word: essential and spirited. Where does such energy come from and how can you emulate it? Experience from the theatre suggests that it happens when you are closely in touch with your passions and interests. You tend to exude vitality when you have a strong personal connection, either with a particular enterprise or with your personal vision, and are able to be a chooser rather than a victim.

A compelling objective or the pressure of deadlines stimulates energy in performers. The last week of rehearsals, for example, demands their total attention. Directors, actors and stage crew will often put in days without sleep to get the show ready for the

'Actors have much in common with taxi drivers. After each run we put up a "for hire" sign and always fear that we may never get another fare.'
Ralph Richardson, actor

opening. It's hard to sustain this level of energy over time; indeed, it would be dangerous to do so. Nevertheless, regularly practising working at this level of vitality helps produce stamina and energy.

Performers often have this energy naturally, but they sustain it by accepting that they have to alternate between intense activity and complete relaxation. In a company you are likely to feel the same. It is very hard to keep the fires of initiative burning if you work in a culture that is debilitating or negative. Then burn-out, cynicism and a tendency to fatalism eventually take their toll.

So where do such resilience, optimism and sheer refusal to quit come from?

Take the case of one of our founding associates, an actor called Eric Ray Evans who ran many of our presentation skills and leadership programmes. In mid-1999 he led his final workshop in which all the evaluation sheets praised his amazing energy and vitality. Participants were unaware that he was undergoing treatment for cancer at the time and he died a month later. Yet Ray managed his energy and dealt with his emotions responsibly and productively – to the point of inspiring his participants.

What Ray had, among other qualities, was absolute commitment to what he was doing, a driving desire to contribute to his 'audience', a continual appetite to develop his craft and a huge heart. The theatre has many examples of performers like Ray, suffering incredible ailments yet able to raise their energy because the show must go on. Actors call this driving passion 'Dr Theatre'.

A balanced lifestyle with a mix of relaxation and activity, plus a healthy diet and regular exercise, all contribute to your vitality. There is no alternative to this sort of commitment to your own well-being. There is also a strong link between energy and emotion. People who appear tired, listless and sapped of vitality usually turn out to be miserable in their work or unhappy in some other area of their life. They have energy, but much of it dissipates into simply

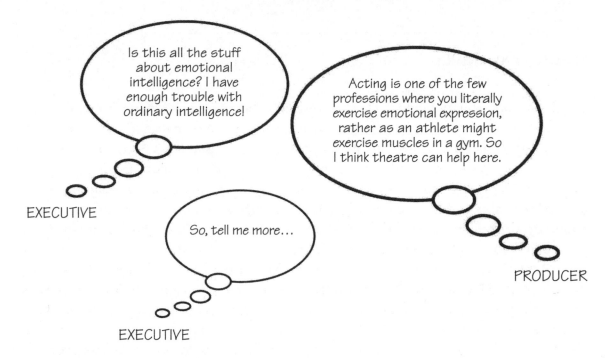

coping. So the next crucial part of the skill set for using personal talent is the ability to handle and express your feelings.

Express your feelings

Recent work by Daniel Goleman on emotional intelligence merely confirms what others, including Einstein, believed, namely that there are many 'intelligences'. Those who can access more than their cerebral intelligence tend to have the most vibrancy. Theatre and therapy are possibly the only two arenas where feelings are explored in any depth.

    Children confirm the strong relationship between emotion and energy. They express themselves through play and in doing so seem to have boundless energy. As we grow older, though, we tend to channel much of our energy into suppressing emotions rather than expressing them. This effort at containment merely depletes our energy.

'I should say the most important elements of acting are feeling and timing. I understand it's the same in many walks of life.'
John Gielgud, actor

EMOTION AND ENERGY

Developmental work around vitality and releasing energy usually focuses on enabling people to express, rather than suppress, their passion or other feelings. Our experience working with countless people has shown us that they can suddenly become more energized and alive when connected to their feelings. Getting something 'off your chest' can indeed be like taking a weight off your shoulders. And the purpose of these exercises (for non-actors) is to gain mastery over your emotional understanding so that you can express your feelings appropriately. It is not an invitation to splurge them over other people in the form of a primitive rant or rage.

Acting requires performers to study nuances and shades of different feelings, and then to practise expressing different levels. There are many processes that you can use to focus on expressing levels of a particular feeling. Take anger or fear, for instance. Try going up and down the 'scales' and practise expressing levels of feeling, increasing and decreasing a little each time. Actors also use 'sense memory' to portray a character's emotional state. This involves recalling and connecting with your own experience of a feeling from your personal history. Such a process can be a cathartic release for many people, as we let go buried feelings from the past, although such work is best done with a qualified facilitator.

'The real actor has a direct line to the collective heart.'
Bette Davis, actor

Does it really matter whether you share your feelings or not? Does it affect individual performance? Certainly, for some managers, sharing feelings seems the stuff of nightmares! After all, you cannot quantify or control feelings and once they are out in the open, almost anything might happen. The work on emotional intelligence, however, confirms what those working in the theatre have long known: for individuals to perform at their best, they need to be skilled in their emotional awareness and expression.

Identifying feelings, let alone talking about them or measuring them, can be difficult since they are hidden backstage in each person's 'inner theatre'. Even so, they unconsciously affect how we

HOW DO YOU FEEL TODAY?

An idea Ricardo Semler used to develop emotional awareness in Semco was to ask people arriving for work to choose a coloured card to indicate how they were feeling that day. One colour indicated that the person was in a bad mood, another that they were in a good mood and so on.

In MLA, we used a whiteboard where people would draw a picture or a symbol expressing how they felt that day, with perhaps a comment alongside. The idea stemmed from a team meeting when members said that they wanted a quick way of finding out a bit more about what was going on with their colleagues.

Like all ideas, after a while this transformed into other ways of achieving the same end. Very rarely do we find ideas like this continuing for ever. It's really important to keep reviewing them.

There are theatrical methods for usefully and safely exploring people's feelings both in workshops and the workplace. They normally start with something that you can do right now.

For example, stop and take a deep breath. How are you feeling? See if you can go beyond a bland 'fine' or 'OK'. Delve a little deeper and see what the feeling is below the surface. You may be experiencing a general sense of well-being, or there may be underlying anxiety.

This is the start of a process of exploration to bring your feelings out. While they are left uncovered, they tend to affect your actions without you knowing. These techniques bring feelings safely to the surface where they can be recognized for what they are: a healthy way to add creativity, honesty and self-expression to a relationship.

How are you feeling right now? Explore at www.maynardleigh.co.uk/feelings.html.

go about our daily lives. Encouraging people to express their feelings about what is happening around them actively helps to create a sense of involvement in a company. Sharing feelings brings people closer to each other because they form deeper and stronger relationships, which are inextricably bound up with outstanding performance. Perhaps this was less true when organizations were simpler organisms, but now their sheer complexity and interconnectedness place relationships at the heart of performance management.

Outstanding performers are in touch with their own feelings and know how they affect others. This experience gives actors ways to interpret feelings and to know when articulating these will be either worthwhile or damaging. Those without such awareness cannot easily manage their own moods. Instead, they are run by suppressed emotions.

Being sensitive to how others feel means that you can help them perform better. It is not merely cathartic when people feel 'heard' through successfully sharing their feelings, it also counteracts unhealthy tendencies to bad mouth, play politics, gossip and manipulate that undermine both individual and corporate performance. Such expertise with feelings is the basis of social intelligence. What is encouraging is that it is certainly learnable.

Use humour

Hal Rosenbluth, chief executive of Rosenbluth International, one of the world's largest travel management companies, insists that 'if executives take themselves too seriously it intimidates others'. It is no coincidence that many political extremists have little or no sense of humour. Rosenbluth uses his playfulness to invite feedback from staff. Rather than data analysis and attitude studies, he adopts unusual initiatives that include the 'Crayola survey', in which staff are invited to send him crayon drawings depicting their feelings about the company.

'An actor must go through the emotions in a night that some people only go through two or three times in their lives, at weddings, funerals and at the side of deathbeds.'
Rip Torn, actor

'Common sense and a sense of humour are the same thing, moving at different speeds. A sense of humour is just common sense, dancing.'
Clive James, writer

Your sense of humour is as individual as a fingerprint. You may not crack jokes or rush around playing the fool, but humour used sensitively and appropriately can allow you to express yourself, as well as helping others work well. In his book *Funny Business*, Jean-Louis Barsoux argues, 'Humour puts the audience in a relaxed and warm frame of mind, in which it is more attentive of what is being said. In business, team leaders often use it to gain attention, bind the group together and promote performance.'

While many people in business are suspicious of emotional expression, they normally mean those situations involving anger and upset. Yet perhaps the most familiar feeling expressed in most workplaces is laughter. Science is only now demonstrating what the entertainment industry has long known, that humour is good for you. Smiling and laughter, for instance, produce chemicals in the body that have direct health benefits. If you readily laugh and smile you will probably have more energy and live longer than those who don't. Humour can lift morale and improve people's spirits.

What exactly is a good sense of humour? It is mainly keeping things in perspective, debunking pomposity or reducing complexity to a simple observation. This is as much a skill as being able to analyse spreadsheets or make sense of company accounts. On the whole the really great performers, whether on stage or in business, invariably possess it. It's about seriously committing to your work without taking yourself too seriously!

'Humour is the shortest distance between two people.'
Victor Borge, entertainer

'I was irrevocably betrothed to laughter, the sound of which has always seemed to me the most civilized music in the world.'
Peter Ustinov, actor/writer/director

Focus your attention

Star performers have a great ability to focus. On the one hand this means *flexibility*, how quickly you can change from one focus to another; and on the other it implies *intensity*, the level of concentration brought to the task.

Often our inner world is so busy that it is hard to be aware of what's really happening around us. We are full of our own

FUN AT WORK

Here are the results of a brainstorm on how a team felt it could have more fun:

★ Groups create limericks about the company and give a prize for the best one.

★ Put wind-up clockwork toys on each desk – when they're wound up and let go, who do they remind you of?

★ Share a skill: have lunchtime sessions where people who have a skill can teach others, e.g. tap dancing, juggling, knitting, origami, watercolour painting, massage.

★ Have a service day – people take turns to serve drinks like a butler.

★ Write a group story – each person writes a sentence and emails it to another person, who adds a sentence and sends it on. Read the final result out at a team meeting.

★ Organize a lunchtime tiddlywinks competition.

★ Ask everyone to bring in a picture of themselves as a baby. Post them on a wall and ask people to guess who they are.

★ Take a photo of everyone as they arrive at work. Post the results in the foyer.

★ Come in wearing your most outrageous clothes.

★ Offer a prize for the funniest joke submitted about the company.

★ Invite a class from a nearby school to come and explain how they'd run the business.

★ For a morning no one can make any statements, only ask questions.

★ Challenge everyone to come to work for one day by a different route.

★ Set up a one-day car pool – everyone gets to be taken home or take someone home.

★ Have a wine and cheese tasting session at the end of the day.

★ Celebrate someone who deserves some accolades with an un-birthday cake at lunch or teatime, and have hats and balloons as well.

★ If public address systems are used office-wide, broadcast a song sung by one or several of the staff's children.

★ On a wet day, defy the weather – pretend you're working in the Caribbean, have fruit cocktails, music playing, dress in brightly coloured clothes etc.

★ Have a 'hand-swap' hour. Right-handed people can only use their left, and vice versa.

★ Everyone chooses an accent and speaks in that accent for a day.

★ Bring in lots of old magazines – do a group collage on a theme in the company.

I've heard that actors are told never to perform on stage with animals. Why is that? Is it because they're unpredictable and might suddenly do something embarrassing?

EXECUTIVE

Possibly. But mostly it's because animals are invariably watchable. They are not self-conscious, full of inner thinking, or busy with trying to prove themselves. Instead, they are simply present – in the moment, aware of what is happening around them. They have real stage presence!

PRODUCER

thoughts. Even as you are reading this book, the voice inside you is producing a running commentary, full of associations, judgements and fantasies. If you don't think you have such a voice, it's probably talking to you at this very moment saying, 'I haven't got a voice in my head.'

People talk of certain actors having 'stage presence'. This is not some magical quality of only famous, charismatic figures. It is in fact a form of intense focus, based on the ability to be fully present – a heightened consciousness where you are aware of everything that is going on. Film director John Boorman explains, 'Presence means exactly that. What all good actors have in common is concentration, the ability to focus all of their attention, intellectually and emotionally, into the character and the scene. Most of us are always partly somewhere else, thinking of what will, or what has happened, allowing part of oneself to stand back and observe the situation instead of being totally in it and of it.'

To be a star performer you somehow have to create what is needed 'right now', to improvise, which stems from having an intense focus on the present situation. In both the theatre and

'I think you have to be schizoid three different ways to be an actor. You've got to be three different people. You have to be a human being. Then you have to be the character you're playing. And on top of that you've got to be the guy sitting out there in Row 10, watching yourself and judging yourself.'
George C. Scott, actor

FOCUS OF ATTENTION

So what exactly can you do to enhance your ability to be present? First, start by bringing your attention to what's happening now. Secondly, really listen without planning what to say when your turn comes. Listen with a clear purpose, mentally checking: 'Am I hearing anything that will move us on? How can I contribute to that?'

Thirdly, to be fully present stay conscious of your feelings and be willing to use these to guide decisions. Fourthly, act as if every single moment is different. For example, many people talk about 'every minute being an opportunity to move the business on'. In that sense you could be doing what every good actor does in rehearsal, on stage and in performance.

Finally, meditation provides useful exercises to help the mind focus. They allow you to become more aware of how your thoughts come and go and how you grow attached to them. Many of us find it incredibly difficult to discipline or focus our minds. It does take practice.

'For a concert to be good I have to be in an ecstatic state of consciousness – sensitivity taken to the greatest possible extreme, so I'm aware of every tiny, tiny micro detail.'
Keith Jarrett,
jazz improviser

business, unless you are truly alert and living in the moment, you cannot easily improvise.

Stage presence applies off stage too. After a chance meeting with the film star Vincent Price, the person concerned marvelled: 'As he shook my hand, it was as if he had crossed the Atlantic to visit me personally.' People who are present seem approachable and open to relationships. Exploring this ability, a team headed by sociologist Robert Bellah suggested that we use our psychic energy through paying attention. This determines the kind of self we are cultivating, the kind of person we are learning to be. When we are giving our full attention to something, when we are really attending, we are calling on all our resources of intelligence, feeling and moral sensitivity.

Actors often exude this quality because it is necessary for their jobs. Broadly, they need to be highly sensitive and aware of everything happening around them: their fellow actors, the audience, the set. The very job of being a professional performer offers daily practice in developing heightened awareness.

Communicate

Michael Caine was playing a role on stage where the character didn't speak throughout a scene. He felt rather at a loose end with nothing to do, until the director gave him the following note: 'Your character is *choosing* not to speak; he is too busy listening.' This allowed Caine to be more active in the scene, knowing that he was contributing something vital.

Jack Lemmon said of his colleague Walter Matthau: 'He acts with you, not at you.' Lemmon explained: 'There are some actors who simply listen to the words rather than listening to the person. Walter always listens to the person.'

The importance of listening cannot be under-estimated. We often work with teams who simply never listen to each other and yet wonder why they have unsupportive relationships.

Communication always involves other people and to do it well your attention has to be fully on the other person. This is the starting point, both for listening and for talking. In fact, many conversations go wrong because of how people do or don't listen. And sadly we often don't listen, we merely nod while we are planning what to say when it's our turn.

A study conducted in 1967 by psychologist Albert Mehrabian concluded that communication is 7 per cent verbal, 38 per cent vocal, and 55 per cent non-verbal. The *verbal* is the words used. The *vocal* refers to the sound, whether intonation or accent. And the *non-verbal* is all about body language, including gesture, posture and expression. You could remember this as words, music and dance.

Even if we don't entirely accept the ratios involved, communication certainly becomes more effective when congruence and

'Acting is all about listening and reacting. It's about being there with the other person. It's not a trick; it's a reality. You convert yourself from a person who's pretending into a person who is. By honestly being there.'
Harrison Ford, actor

'Listening is being able to be changed by the other person. It's not hearing them, it's not waiting for your cue, it's not when are they going to stop so I can talk. It's letting them in.'
Alan Alda,
actor/writer/director

ACTIVE LISTENING

Listening is an activity with purpose. Actors need to know what their character is listening for. What are they trying to hear? It is all about focus again. Where is the character's focus of attention?

Notice where your attention is as you listen. What are you listening for? Are you looking for opportunities to make your point; to mock the person who is speaking; to seek agreement; to remember the facts and figures someone is providing; to spot something you can argue against; to hear how you can support the person; to undermine them; to try to add value to their ideas; or what?

The more you can listen with a positive purpose, the more likely you are to be effective in your communication.

consistency exist between these three areas. To paraphrase a song, 'It ain't what you say, it's the way that you say it.' Actors are trained in both vocal and physical techniques. Why not potential star performers in business?

Our voice should reflect our true feelings. It is an expression of who we are. It is the authentic sound of the self.

Understand character

Anthony Sher is an accomplished painter as well as one of the UK's foremost classical actors. In considering the link between both these artistic endeavours, he explains how actors make sense of people: 'If I was to do a drawing of you, I'd be observing things about you and sketching lines on paper. If I were playing you as a character I'd do the same thing, except I'd be using my body and voice instead of lines on paper. I think that's what all actors do. They sketch characters and colour them in with themselves.'

'Suit the action to the word, and the word to the action.'
Hamlet,
William Shakespeare

When building an interesting character on stage, actors are curious about what is different and distinctive about the person they are portraying, rather than how they fit into a pre-determined pigeonhole. They try to empathize, rather than criticize. Any of us who want to develop productive relationships also need such social intelligence. And that starts by being curious about each person we work with.

However, what we perceive is affected by our history and our past experiences. We see through a fog of beliefs, prejudices, interpretations, judgements, interests and blind spots. It is hard to see people as they truly are, untainted by our assumptions about them, let alone in fresh and sympathetic ways. Actors start by simply observing. They are people watchers.

Exercises in trying to understand another person are especially useful when we are faced with difficulties such as disputes, conflicts, arguments, or simply feeling that we're not working particularly well together. Sometimes our personal performance gets affected by so-called problem people. The best way to start dealing with such aggravating relationships is by trying to put ourselves in the other person's shoes, just as an actor might in playing a part. We often know surprisingly little about such people. We may even know more about what makes our computers work than about our colleagues.

Turn talent into performance

It is one thing for us to have a talent, another to unleash it and realize our full potential. When we bring a latent capability to fruition, it is like bringing one of those 'magic eye' pictures into its full 3D brilliance. Initially invisible, the complete picture is there all the time, only requiring a mental and creative shift to recognize it. Such realization of talent can be achieved in various ways, for instance when we learn and develop on the job, when we face new

> 'It's my body. That's what I work with.'
> Gerard Depardieu, actor

> 'I could sit all day in a telephone booth on 42nd Street and just watch the people pass by. Human behaviour has always fascinated me. Actors have to know how much spit you've got in your mouth and where the weight of your elbows is.'
> Marlon Brando, actor

BECOME AN EXPERT IN BODY LANGUAGE

There is more nonsense written about body language than about almost any other aspect of communication. Most stems from a fruitless rule-bound approach, which defines certain gestures as always revealing fixed attitudes. For example: arms crossed means you are defended; touching your mouth means you are lying. This leads to so-called body language experts instructing you to 'always hold your hands in a "steeple" position when presenting; always place your thumb and index finger on your chin while listening'. This sort of approach is superficial and tends to turn human beings into automatons.

The actor's approach is different, treating each person as unique. They observe people and use their own intelligence to intuit what the posture or gesture means. You can use this technique as well. When you see someone hold their body in a certain way, try to replicate it yourself, as if you were acting the role of that person in a play. By inhabiting their expression in this way, you will normally elicit some understanding of why they behave in the way they do. It will help you 'read' their body language.

This approach not only assists you in understanding others, it also helps you to become more aware of your own body language. You will notice why you move or gesture in a certain way and spot potentially misleading mannerisms.

When people who are connected to themselves and their passions communicate, their physical expression works naturally for them. So rather than trying to learn 'rules' about body language, use your intuition and try speaking from the heart.

KNOW YOUR COLLEAGUES BETTER

Insight into people and their potential for outstanding performance starts with observation and is fuelled by curiosity. Replace being judgemental by switching to being curious and start to understand others better.

For example, summon up a mental picture of someone you work with, such as a colleague with whom you regularly have contact. Let's assume it's a woman. Ask yourself the following questions about her:

★   Why does she do what she does?
★   Why does she move the way she does?
★   What are her characteristic actions or speech?
★   What is she feeling?
★   What does she want?
★   What isn't being said?
★   How do her words differ from her actions?
★   What are these actions telling me?
★   How would I feel in her shoes?
★   How am I similar to her?
★   How am I different to her?
★   What motivates her?
★   What would be a challenge for her?
★   What would she really need?
★   What would be a treat for her?
★   What's going on in her life outside of work at the moment?
★   How does this affect the way she behaves?

DEVELOPMENT INITIATIVES TO NURTURE TALENT

There are many actions you can take to accelerate your own and other people's development. Here are just a few of them:

★ *Coaching and mentoring*: receiving guidance from internal or external 'experts' to support development.
★ *Topic seminars*: holding short, internal seminars on relevant areas of knowledge or expertise.
★ *Shared learning*: allowing time for people to share their knowledge and expertise.
★ *Job shadowing*: spending a half-day or day alongside a colleague to understand the scope of their job.
★ *Job swapping*: taking over another person's job for a fixed period.
★ *New challenges*: taking on new responsibilities, particularly ones that are a bit scary.
★ *Personal budgets*: allocating an amount of money to each person to be spent on an area of personal development.
★ *Team meetings*: practising new skills or sharing experiences and knowledge.
★ *Outside stimuli*: exploring best practice elsewhere by visiting other organizations and seeing how they conduct their affairs.
★ *Attending workshops*: participating in learning events that allow experimentation with new skills.

challenges, or as the result of receiving coaching and mentoring. Another route is through attending development workshops that allow us to practise and experience new forms of behaviour in a safe yet challenging environment.

But not all development workshops help people grow and deliver dramatic performance. Many rely on traditional academic methods – 'talk and chalk' – encouraging participants to be cerebral and retreat into the abstract, staying removed from the real-life experience. Much so-called training merely teaches people how to maintain the status quo, rather than how to bring about personal change.

Theatre and film directors approach their work with actors as a dynamic and creative experience. Development in companies that unlocks people's potential is similar, focusing on what we call 'whole self learning'. Just as no one learns to ride a bike by reading a manual, in whole self learning we mainly learn by doing. It uses all our preferred learning styles and is a holistic approach, integrating left and right brain; mental and physical; heart and mind; visual and oral; kinaesthetic and feeling; intuitive and reasoning – just like theatre. How do we know this works? Because this is precisely how actors rehearse plays and it is also how children learn and develop. It is both natural and effective.

To change your own behaviour as part of striving to be a star performer, you will need to be rather like an actor in rehearsal, continually stepping into the unknown. To interpret a character and discover what is really going on in a scene, actors get on their feet and start adopting behaviour that may be alien to them. They experiment and reveal options and choices for new action. For this to occur, certain conditions must exist and they are exactly the same as in corporate development events:

★ *Honesty*: openness about behaviour and feelings.
★ *An affirming atmosphere*: creating a positive place in which to risk and grow.
★ *Creativity*: offering interesting and inspiring behavioural choices.
★ *Play*: making the experience fun.
★ *Relevant*: related to the participants' real needs.

Whole self learning is a visceral experience, releasing a person's natural aptitude to do something. People embody their learning by acting it out. If we want to get our personal act together, we need this sort of approach.

Rather like a theatre director working with an actor, a skilfully run learning event provides stimulating ideas for new behaviour that individuals can try out. Because these ideas are creative they are often intriguing and fun, bypassing people's defences. Instead of breaking people down and building them up again, the approach is more holistic and humane. People receive ideas that offer a new way of acting and being and find that it is safe to try them. As somebody once remarked: 'It is often easier to act your way into a new way of thinking than to think your way into a new way of acting.'

On the next few pages, Darren Facey, European client manager at Hewlett-Packard, describes being a participant on a learning event and putting a challenging opportunity to good effect.

In June 2001 I visited Stratford-upon-Avon on a self-leadership, motivational business course, called 'UBU' (or You Be You!). I couldn't understand the rationale for running this programme in the current IT climate. I thought, 'Times are tough today. I need to be with customers to help close deals, not waste time on a "self-help" course.' As it turned out it was the best two days' development I have ever had in my 16 years in this industry.

On the first day the workshop leaders greeted us without any material and the room was empty with the curtains drawn. There were no flip charts or projector. We stood looking at each other waiting for something to happen, but it didn't. Every time we asked what was happening we were given the reply, 'What do you want to happen and what would you like from this course?' It seemed so alien to us but the idea was for us to be self-driven, to structure our own destiny, to think outside the box and reach for the stars.

At the end of the first day, we were set a challenge: to write down ten risks that did not break the law, and perform one of them before the next day. The risk had to be one that stretched you as a person so you felt out of your comfort zone, and was not too life threatening. I had the idea to contact the Royal Shakespeare Company and see if I could be a thespian for the evening.

Five of the team went to the theatre to see *Twelfth Night.* As we paid for our tickets I asked who the director of the play was and I was told it was Lindsay Posner. I asked if she was in that evening, as I needed to talk to her urgently. I was politely told, 'She is a he, sir.' Great start, I thought.

It turned out that Mr Posner would not be in, as the play had been running for a while. Undeterred and with the curtain about to go up, I made a last-ditch attempt. I found the name of the stage manager, Katie Vine, dashed round the theatre to the stage door, introduced myself to a very nice woman on the door and explained my plight. She looked at me in amazement, but said that there was nothing she could do now as the curtain was going up: 'Come back in the interval and we will see.'

At the interval I ran to the stage door. Katie Vine was there and she said right away that I could be part of the team for one night. I was overjoyed. I thanked the woman on the stage door and was led into 'backstage land'.

My first task was to initiate the announcement telling the audience that there were five minutes left of the interval and to return to their seats. Part one complete, my adrenaline was beginning to rise. At this point I was introduced to Mark Hadfield who played Feste. He immediately produced three tambourines and said, 'Now, you can juggle, right? We need you to go on stage and juggle these three tambourines at the start of the next act.' My heart stopped with fright. It was just then when I saw he was not being serious, luckily.

My next task was to become a hairdresser. I was introduced to Guy Henry who played Malvolio. My task was to produce a kiss curl at the front of Malvolio's hair. As I was given the curling tongs, I had to point out that I had never done this before. This made Guy feel totally relaxed, as you can imagine, especially when I pointed out that I could smell burning. At last with the tongs removed I saw my design, which was rather splendid for a complete novice.

I was then introduced to Gabrielle Sanders, the deputy stage manager, who effectively runs the show, and she gave me a quick overview of her incredibly complex role. The curtain went up for the second half. My first task here was, at a signal, to press button 74 to instruct the actor to walk on from stage left. This may seem a simple task, but I suddenly felt like an air traffic controller where one mistake could be disastrous. I tried to compose myself, waiting for the nod, with my finger hovering over button 74. Finally the nod came, I pressed with conviction and on came Sir Toby Belch, played by Barry Stanton, whose comedic belch and vomit scene had so impressed me in the first act.

My final and most nerve-racking task was to cue the soldiers to march on to the stage from both sides, but the twist was that I had to follow the script. Gabrielle showed me the switches and indicated where we were in the play and sat back. My cue word was 'Awake'. My fingers were poised over switches 62 and 64, while my eyes followed the scripted dialogue. If I missed this cue, 16 soldiers would not appear – no pressure. In my mind I kept repeating the word, awake, awake, awake, as if I would forget it. I heard the word spoken and, like the bell from a clock, it rang in my head. My action was swift and direct. I looked up to see 16 marching soldiers parade on to the stage. Mission completed. I turned to Gabrielle where we had a brief 'luvvie' moment of congratulations, then I retreated from the pressurized firing line to let her fly the plane once more.

I sat back and enjoyed the rest of the performance, truly appreciating the amount of work that goes on backstage in a production from the RSC. When a play runs smoothly and the actors are very good, you're led to believe that it is not that difficult to produce. This could not be further from the truth. A play like *Twelfth Night* takes 12 weeks of set design, lighting, orchestra, costume, planning and rehearsals to put together. Next time you attend any theatrical performance, please spare a thought for the unseen heroes who dash around behind the scenes, keeping the show going come what may.

What this theatrical experience taught me was how much of a leader I already was. Two other people on the course, stimulated by my experience, stretched themselves even more, taking even bigger risks. The experience also gave me more self-awareness, made me look at problems differently, to think more out of the box and to try to get more of an outside view on issues. It's made me more positive in this close-knit HP environment.

INTERVAL

THE PLOT SO FAR...

In case you arrived late and missed the opening act, here's a synopsis of the story so far.

The opening explored how you can combine the best of business and the best of theatre to understand how to produce dramatic success. This involves getting your act together in three areas: yourself, your team and your organization.

Act I was all about producing outstanding personal performance. The show started with a look at star performance and the importance of individuality. This means accessing your full personal resources and the three vital elements for producing outstanding personal performance:

★   Scene 1: Personal connection – being able to answer the question 'What's in it for me?'
★   Scene 2: Personal power – taking responsibility and being proactive.
★   Scene 3: Personal talent – developing the actor's skill set to embrace dynamic times.

The curtain came down on this act after a look at how talent can be nurtured and released. While we wait for the stage settings to be changed after Act I, our producer and executive adjourn to the bar and reflect on what they have just seen.

As we await the start of Act II, there is time to look behind the scenes at other examples of performance issues.

There are many instances of people transforming their personal effectiveness in order to perform outstandingly. Here are a few scenes from the workplace to illustrate what can happen when people make a commitment to develop.

BEHIND THE SCENES

In which Gordon faces up to his personal performance

It all starts when Fiona of Multibank meets her boss, Raoul.

RAOUL: I have to tell you, Fiona, I really don't think you're performing at your best right now. Somehow, you seem to lack vitality and I notice you're letting things slip.

FIONA: I know, I know. Look, to be honest, I agree with you. I really can do better than this.

RAOUL: So what's going on?

FIONA: I suppose the truth is, I don't feel that my work is respected. There's nothing I'm doing that seems particularly exciting or challenging right now. And, umm, while I don't want to dump this on you, I have to say I don't think you're particularly clear about what you expect from me.

RAOUL: Oh. That's news to me! I have to say I wasn't aware of this.

FIONA: Well, I probably should have said earlier. But anyway, I'm telling you now.

RAOUL: Right, I appreciate that. OK, I will endeavour to be clearer in future. In fact, I'll start right now. I need to feel that you are committed and on the ball.

FIONA: I know, fair enough. But I think I've kind of gone off the boil because I don't feel challenged or stretched. I need something to get my teeth into.

RAOUL: Now I know where you stand, I think I may have just the job...

Some months later, Fiona is having a drink with her friend Gordon from Megabank in a local wine bar. She is buying the first round.

GORDON: I really need this. You know, Fi, I've absolutely had it with work.

FIONA: What's the problem? You seemed happy enough last time we spoke.

GORDON: Well, now I feel totally uninspired. When did we last get together – six months ago, was it? Then I was really up for anything. I felt totally engaged and motivated about what I was doing. But now, I honestly couldn't care less.

FIONA: Funny, you know I've just been through a period a bit like that.

GORDON: Really? What did you do?

FIONA: To be honest, it wasn't me, it was Raoul. A good bit of performance management, I reckon. He confronted me. We had a good chat and he really seemed to listen. I honestly don't think he realized that a lot of it was to do with the way he was managing me. I just wasn't being stretched.

GORDON: You're right! I think that's exactly what it's about. I don't feel acknowledged and I don't feel challenged.

FIONA: You could always do something about it.

GORDON: Yes, you're right. I could.

There is a lot that can be done to ensure that people perform at their best:

★ Personal performance needs attention.

★ Gordon and Fiona need to be responsible for their own performance.

★ That means continually monitoring and reviewing how they are doing.

★ Once they realize that they are not satisfied, they need to take swift action.

★ Equally, both Raoul and Gordon's manager need continually to emphasize the level of performance they expect.

★ Jointly, they need to collaborate on exploring what keeps Gordon and Fiona feeling challenged and excited in their work.

In which Hanna makes an inspirational speech

After a particularly turbulent year at her magazine publishing company Senior Executive, Hanna rises to give the opening speech at the annual conference.

'Welcome. It's really good to see you all here today.

'I won't mince my words, I want to get straight to the point. Last year was a tough year. We had to make a lot of very difficult decisions. I know you've all worked incredibly hard to get us through.

'But the good news is, the worst is over. The work we did last year has put us in a really good position to be successful in the coming year. Everything we did was to make sure we are ready. Ready to work together efficiently, ready to compete in the hugely difficult market environment and, most importantly, ready to win.'

What was the audience's reaction to these inspiring words? Here's what some of them said afterwards:

★   Didn't believe it.
★   It's all right for her, we're the ones who have suffered most.
★   I think she'll be gone within the year.
★   Big disappointment.
★   She didn't look comfortable with the way forward.

What went wrong? Why did Hanna's words fall on such deaf ears and engender such a negative response?

Hanna's inner dialogue, the voice in her head, kept commenting all the while she was speaking, inexorably communicating itself through voice and body. No wonder the audience picked up a mixed message from her. Here's what Hanna was really saying under the surface:

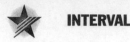

THIS IS WHAT THE AUDIENCE HEARS	HANNA'S INNER DIALOGUE
Welcome.	Here we go, into the lion's den. Phew, they look so hostile.
It's really good to see you all here today.	I wish it was.
I won't mince my words, I want to get straight to the point.	How can I get this over with as quickly as possible?
Last year was a tough year.	Worse for me than it was for you.
We had to make a lot of very difficult decisions.	Sacking people is the pits. Mind you, they deserved it.
I know you've all worked incredibly hard to get us through.	If you had, we wouldn't be in the mess we're in now.
But the good news is, the worst is over.	I hope.
The work we did last year has put us in a really good position to be successful in the coming year.	With this lot?
Everything we did was to make sure we are ready.	Everything we did was in desperation!
Ready to work together efficiently, ready to compete in the hugely difficult market environment and, most importantly, ready to win.	Well, now we at least stand a chance – more than we did before I stepped in and shook the place up.
Thank you.	You're supposed to be applauding!

Before giving an important speech, Hanna needs to get her thinking straight. But it is not enough simply to change her thoughts. 'Positive thinking' alone becomes mere pretence. She needs to be able to believe in what she is saying. For that to happen there is work Hanna can do before she stands up to speak, so that she communicates her true message.

Some actions she can take:

★ Have discussions with people about their experiences over the last year. How tough was it for them? How do they feel now? How have they contributed to the change?

★   Really debate the strategy so that she is convinced it's the best option.
★   Build alliances with staff so that she knows she's got some 'champions' in the audience.
★   Make sure that enough people are behind the new plans.
★   Rehearse her presentation with a colleague who can play devil's advocate for her.
★   Check the speech for anything she can't truly support.

Then her outer and inner dialogue can complement each other and she can present a coherent and consistent message to her audience:

THIS IS WHAT THE AUDIENCE HEARS	HANNA'S INNER DIALOGUE
Welcome.	OK, I'm prepared. I'm looking forward to exciting them about future opportunities.
It's really good to see you all here today.	I know these people, they are my colleagues.
I won't mince my words, I want to get straight to the point.	Let's get on with it.
Last year was a tough year. We had to make a lot of very difficult decisions.	It was painful – for all of us. We all had to do some rotten stuff.
I know you've all worked incredibly hard to get us through.	As I look around I can see Tom and Rita and Ulli and Gareth and I know how committed they've been.
But the good news is, the worst is over.	What a relief it's over and we can move on.
The work we did last year has put us in a great position to be successful in the coming year.	I really believe that the new strategy gives us a great chance.
Everything we did was to make sure we are ready.	We've got a platform to move forward.
Ready to work together efficiently, ready to compete in the hugely difficult market environment and, most importantly, ready to win.	If I think about our vision for how it could be, I reckon we can do it.

In which Helen learns a new approach to managing her emotions

Helen is meeting with three colleagues. As often happens, she is disappointed by their missed deadlines and she interrogates each of them, one by one.

HELEN: What do you mean, another delay? (*Raising her voice*) You really are impossible. You're two weeks behind schedule now and every time I ask you what the problem is you come out with a load of excuses. I don't want excuses. (*Screaming*) I want *results*!

Helen is now flushed with anger. She is on the point of exploding. It is not the first time.

That evening, Helen confides in a colleague about her performance at the meeting.

JOHN: So how often does this happen?
HELEN: Too often. I get totally out of control. I try to contain my anger and frustration but it wells up inside of me. I just want to kill.
JOHN: Have you ever thought about treating your colleagues as if they were clients?
HELEN: What do you mean?
JOHN: Well, we tend not to get so plugged in with our clients. In fact, if they have a problem we approach it with curiosity, not judgement. Sometimes it takes the sting out of the interaction.
HELEN: That sounds like a good idea. I can try that.
JOHN: Also, I think you spend a lot of time trying to control your feelings. Knowing you, that just means that you're bottling them up. They're bound to come out later. If you actually noticed them quicker and just said how you feel, that might stop you exploding like a pressure cooker. And then, if you were curious about why the problem existed, you might get better results.

While expressing feelings with passion is an important part of being personally effective, losing control is not. John's advice is a way forward for Helen. There are other things she can do too:

★   Recognize feelings 'in the moment'.
★   If she expresses feelings early and tells the truth about them, they tend to be less charged.
★   Deal with the problem rather than attacking the people.
★   Trying to understand and work out what's going on means that Helen is involved in the problem and its solution, rather than staying on the outside simply being demanding.

Helen is once again meeting with her colleagues. This time, though, she simply tells the truth about her feelings, exploring the issues with curiosity rather than anger.

HELEN: What do you mean, another delay? Look, I can't tell you how cross I feel when this happens. I also feel deeply disappointed, as I think I've already been incredibly understanding about previous delays. (*Taking a deep breath and speaking in a calm way*) Now, come on, let's get down to solving this one instead of simply excusing it. What could possibly be done differently to speed up the process?

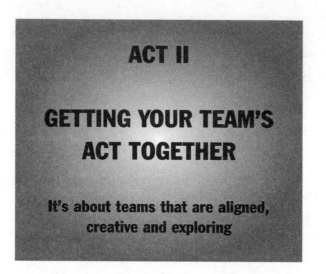

ACT II

GETTING YOUR TEAM'S ACT TOGETHER

It's about teams that are aligned, creative and exploring

It's all very well performing outstandingly myself, but that's useless if my colleagues aren't working as a team. I want to know the secret of dramatic team performance.

Executive

As they wait for the curtain to rise on Act II, the company executive and his producer friend discuss the show so far.

EXECUTIVE: I liked Act I. It got me really thinking. But let me ask you a question: What keeps you awake at night?

PRODUCER: That's rather personal.

EXECUTIVE: No, what I mean is, if you wake up and your mind starts churning away at something, what is it? What do you worry about?

PRODUCER: I suppose it depends on whether I've got a show opening. Then all my attention is on its success. And you?

EXECUTIVE: Competitive advantage. That's what consumes me. I know I need to be at my best and the same goes for all those around me. But I reckon there's something else that'll give us the edge.

PRODUCER: Ah, you've got to be talking teams.

EXECUTIVE: Teams – ugh! I've never seen so much time wasted in boring, ineffectual meetings and consultations than when there's a team involved. What's the old adage: a meeting is a place where they take minutes and waste hours? You're not advocating management by committee, I hope.

PRODUCER: No way. But there's a big difference between a team and a committee. And if you want exceptional results, then several heads used properly have got to be better than one.

EXECUTIVE: Maybe, although it's so tedious. I've always found teams really hard work.

PRODUCER: In the theatre teams have to form incredibly quickly. You've often only got a few weeks' rehearsal before you open the production. So getting an ensemble performing well together is the prime focus. I tell you, it doesn't have to take for ever.

★ ★ ★ ★ ★

Meanwhile, bells have sounded and the members of the audience have taken their seats, ready for the curtain to rise on Act II, which dramatizes the three essential elements needed in order to transform team performance.

The plot for this act revolves around the three factors that make an ACE team:

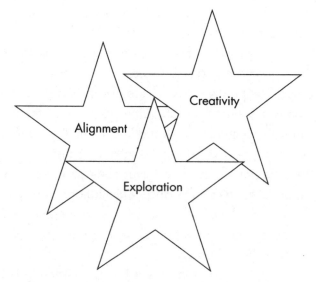

So the drama unfolds in the following way:

★   Scene 1 – *Team alignment*: a collective commitment to teamworking, with people sharing the same values, going in the same direction, with clear roles and tight organization.

★   Scene 2 – *Team creativity*: the group has creative energy, people feel fully used and bring all of themselves to the enterprise, especially their curiosity and sense of wonder in a playful environment.

★   Scene 3 – *Team exploration*: with an adventurous spirit the team takes its performance out into the world, adding value to stakeholders, learns from successes and failures, and celebrates.

SCENE 1
TEAM ALIGNMENT

When is a team not a team? When it's a group, a committee or a working party. Even when they have it in their title, teams are often only that in name, merely a group of individuals attending meetings together. Most sales teams, for example, are nothing of the kind. Instead, they consist of individuals with their own targets, working competitively against each other. Up close these pretend teams contain people who hoard leads and ideas, act in opposition not in concert, and the company rewards them only as individuals.

Similarly, there are many so-called executive teams that come together to oversee the running of an organization and don't behave like a team. This is mainly because each person tends to run their own division or department and they meet almost reluctantly at an executive level for the sake of coordination and broad policy. While even this requires some sort of teamworking, it will never achieve the excitement of a fully fledged ensemble.

Acting companies gel so quickly in the early stages of rehearsal because each performer knows that they depend totally on their colleagues for success. This interdependency encourages teamworking. The same goes for the corporate environment, where the best teams deliver truly dramatic success.

Have you ever been part of a team grappling to solve a really tricky problem, experiencing all sorts of difficulties and 'stuckness' together? If so, you will know the feeling of being part of something bigger than yourself. And when, after many struggles, you see a solution emerge and enjoy the delight of group performance, then you experience at first hand the value of a team. When teamworking goes well it produces outstanding results, far beyond what any individual can achieve alone. In addition, it engenders feelings of community and camaraderie that encourage the most talented people to stick around.

EVIDENCE OF TEAMWORKING

Consider your own team. How much of its activity is interdependent? Do you work on projects together? Are you dependent on others in the team for your own success? Are your meetings mainly boring or closer to ritual than reality?

Try recalling a recent team success and ask yourself how it came about. Whose idea was it? How did it come to fruition? How did the solution arise?

Great teams are seldom entirely due to just one person. More often they arise from a combined effort. They apply a bit of unscientific magic stemming from many people's input and an immeasurable blend of human chemistry.

'Actors commit so much to the work. It is so important to them that acting always puts you in a life and death situation and fear is a great energy.'
Glenda Jackson, actor

While teams can be highly productive, they can also be extremely hard work. Before you decide to go for the team option, give some time to considering whether you really do want to pay the high price required. Explore the implications and see what it takes. You might conclude that it is in fact not worth it. You only get a team when there is a collective will – not an individual won't.

Real teams depend entirely on there being something personally at stake for each team member. Crudely, it's probably about pain and pleasure. Either there are exciting benefits from being involved or there are acute losses. For actors it could be that their reputation is on the line; or they want to advance their career; or they're in a blockbuster that could earn them a fortune; or it's an artistic stretch; or they are passionate about the subject matter of the play; or they always wanted to play a particular role and this is their chance; or they simply want to avoid the humiliation of audience rejection and critical reviews.

Team members give their commitment when they have a strong investment in the success of the enterprise. Such success governs the ensemble's collective performance and therefore creates powerful alignment. Their investment is not necessarily a

TEAM TABLEAUX

You could use a drama-based technique to identify how aligned your team is. This is sensitive and demands skilful facilitation, so you might need an outside consultant. It highlights problem areas in a very powerful way.

The team members are asked to arrange themselves physically as they see the team relationships to be, and preferably to remain silent while doing so. (You could also use props or simply chairs and tables.) The tableau often displays the team dynamic. People reveal their view of the team by placing themselves in relationship to each other. Some teams don't put the leader in the centre, for instance. Others have certain team members turned away or separate from a core group. Some choose to be on a higher or lower level than others to demonstrate the power relationships. Some stand close or behind others, while some express their frustration and resentment and adopt an aloof or even an aggressive stance. You could perhaps take a photograph.

Then ask team members how they would like the relationships to be. This creates a second tableau. Another photograph records this. The job is then to identify what is needed in the team to move from one to the other.

financial one, although that happens too, as when a team goes for a management buy-out or members take up share options. The essence of personal investment is commitment, not cash. It is turning personal investment into real action and identifiable behaviour.

The best ensembles are built on relationships. Great teams don't have to like each other, but they do have to work together impeccably. In our own development work with teams we often focus on exploring the power of their relationships to go beyond mere competence to deliver star performance.

Alignment is all about relationships and understanding each other, so you've got to get the right mix of people in the first place.

Rouben Mamoulian, a distinguished director of plays and Broadway productions, had smash hits with *Porgy and Bess, Carousel*

GET THE RIGHT TEAM

Rather than sending people off to anonymous assessment centres, why not conduct an 'audition' where you get a chance to experience what it would be like if the person joined your team? Create opportunities for them to spend time with the team, perhaps a morning brainstorming solutions to a problem. Or work on a creative project with them.

Keep a lookout for their teamworking behaviour. Do they listen well and build on other people's ideas? Are they creative? Do they focus their attention on others? Do they add value?

and the long-running *Oklahoma!*. He favoured large casts and spectacular designs. He was famous for his crowd scenes, where even the most insignificant character was three-dimensional. He believed in the ensemble, refusing to allow any actor or production element to dominate. Knowledgeable in all the visual arts, Mamoulian used imagery to align everyone around his picture of what the group must achieve. He worked slowly and continually revised until he was satisfied. This master of team alignment was famous for his ability to remain calm no matter how chaotic the circumstances.

Many theatre directors who have successfully run ensemble companies look for balance in their casts. It is no good having one star performer if it's at the expense of everybody else. There is little space for huge egos who want to dominate. Michael Caine joined Joan Littlewood's Theatre Workshop Company in the 1960s and openly admits to being sacked by her because she felt he was not an ensemble player. And a common actor's joke about big, self-important celebrities is that they need two dressing rooms: one for changing in and one for their ego!

Anthony Sher talks with admiration about his first acting season in Liverpool and the great mix of talent within the team:

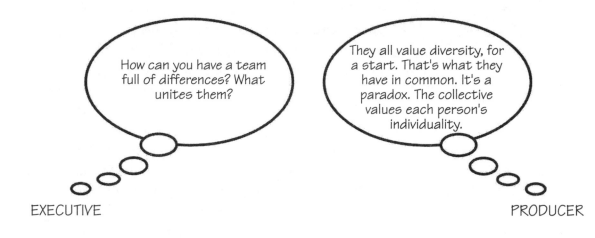

How can you have a team full of differences? What unites them?

They all value diversity, for a start. That's what they have in common. It's a paradox. The collective values each person's individuality.

EXECUTIVE   PRODUCER

'That year at the Everyman was exhilarating. Not only were Jonathan Pryce, Bernard Hill, Alison Steadman, Pete Postlethwaite and Julie Walters in the company, the directors were Alan Dosser and Richard Eyre, and the writers included Alan Bleasdale, Willy Russell and John McGrath. It was one of those golden ages which blesses some theatres from time to time.'

When recruiting, watch out for the tendency to want to employ people just like you. It's a casting issue. The essential principle is the creation of diversity. No theatre production would work with twelve Hamlets in the cast. Diverse teams and companies have a rich culture that enriches everyone. Different people bring different approaches and perspectives.

Respect for this diversity and what each person brings to the team is a key to how people can feel that their individuality is appreciated within the context of the collective.

> 'Eighty per cent of a successful production is in the casting.'
> Lindsay Anderson, director

Support each other

Developing the kind of relationships needed for a team to perform outstandingly is a complex issue, full of subtle stuff that can prove demanding for team leaders, facilitators and companies as a whole. Guidelines for what makes a star-performing team, let alone a list of practical actions, can seem almost facile. Yet so important are teams and the essential requirements for what makes them tick that we feel it is right to share some of what we know works.

In theatre the idea of teams supporting other people tends to be uppermost in everyone's mind. It's a decisive, make-or-break issue. When you gather on the first day of rehearsal, knowing that you have a show to rehearse and present to your customers in, say, three weeks' time, it affects how you go about forming relationships. You also know that you are dependent on these people to support you in your work. Without them you are dead.

FAST RELATIONSHIP BUILDING

An acting company starts relationship building early on, and quickly. There is no lengthy lead time for allowing relationships to develop, so exercises are often used to oil the wheels. Many of these are similar to some of the team-building processes used in the corporate world. However, as the purpose of these techniques is to break through the conventional social barriers, they need to be handled with care. Many so-called icebreakers could better be renamed 'embarrassment generators'.

Yet certain activities allow people, in an enjoyable way, to develop awareness, discover one another, share histories and experiences, and generally get to know each other better. It can take minutes rather than days.

In a separate team-building session, or as a regular agenda item at the team meeting, try out a few of these exercises.

Share your three favourite books; tell your life story in 60 seconds; in pairs spend five minutes finding out ways in which you are similar and ways in which you are different; share your proudest moment; confess your biggest embarrassments or mistakes; describe your best friend; tell your nickname at school.

The important point is to get behind the 'mask' so that team members can start seeing each other properly.

Tune in and trust

TEAM FOCUS

'Tuning in' takes a few minutes and can save hours. It allows group members to focus their attention on the team task ahead, by ensuring that everyone gets a sense of how people are. Each person quickly shares how they feel and if there is anything in the way of them fully contributing to the meeting. Comments might go something like this:

★ I feel really energetic today. I've got a lot on, but I feel on top of it.
★ I'm a bit hung-over, it was my sister's birthday last night. So I'm really trying to concentrate, but give me a nudge if I start drifting.
★ I'm feeling overwhelmed. I'm really behind on the report I'm working on and I'm keen to get back to it. In fact, I'm really angry that it's been dumped on me at the last minute. But I've said it now, so I can let it go for a bit and focus myself here.
★ Watch out! Today I'm raring to go, I really feel up for anything.
★ I'm a bit distracted. My mum's having tests at the hospital today and I'm worried about her.

Once the team has a sense of how each member is, they can relate appropriately and work more effectively together.

Actors know that they cannot produce star performance unless their relationships are strong. It's about making a connection. So an hour or so before the curtain rises for a performance, the best ensembles commonly gather on stage. They may not have seen each other all day so they want to check in with their fellow team members and be together for a while. They do voice exercises or limber up. This helps everyone tune in.

Business teams can benefit from equivalent preparation, their own version of tuning in. This is more likely to happen over coffee or at the start of a meeting. Rather than plunge into the maelstrom of current issues, it really pays to pause, taking time to 'touch base' with each other. This is not about making small talk, though that too can be useful. It is about getting the chemistry right, detecting anything that might stop the group succeeding.

In virtual teams, those that mainly meet electronically through email or video conferences for example, everything depends on constant communication. In a study of 29 global virtual teams, initial communications set the tone for how people related to other for the entire project. These first interactions were seen as crucial to building relationships and creating trust.

Trust happens quickly in theatre teams because the actors know that they depend on each other during performances. So they tend to start by instinctively trusting each other until proven wrong, rather than working from a position of 'prove to me you're trustworthy'.

Most relationships normally need to go through various stages before establishing trust. After the initial attraction phase, based perhaps on shared interests or objectives, there are periods of meeting challenges and maybe weathering storms together. The more intense the group experience, the stronger the relationships. The only difference between theatre and business teams in this respect is that theatre teams generally do this more quickly.

Whether in business or the theatre, star-performing teams establish trust because people talk to each other with respect, which supports and encourages their work together. Respect goes deeper than mere politeness; indeed, sometimes there are sharp words and even anger. It's about showing that you value your colleagues and believe in their contribution, while staying alert for ways to help them perform even better. The crucial element is continuous honest and constructive feedback.

'If the actor does not get the support of his fellow actors, his performance will lack resonance and depth. He will be lured into wrong inflections and wrong rhythms. That is why rapport amongst actors is imperative for the success of the play.'
August Strindberg, playwright

'There is something about combining with a group of people in a common cause. It is a kind of intimacy that you feel, even though you don't know each other very well.'
Lynn Redgrave, actor

TRUST

Early rehearsals in acting companies often involve trust exercises to accelerate the process. Most are physical, which quickly gets to the heart of the matter. They might involve mirroring exercises, or being led around blindfolded, or diving off tables and trusting that your colleagues will catch you. These dramatic displays of risk, care and reliability help short-cut the normal, longer process that develops trust.

This means that right from the word go, people are taking risks and supporting one another. Each performer must be scrupulous in their attention and care for the others. One slip and trust is diminished. This is particularly necessary if the rehearsal or performance process will demand revealing raw emotion or working together in a physical way.

Although such exercises are used in workshops, you can help your team quickly form trust by getting its members to be sensitive to each other as they take risks, or really listen and support each other when tackling an emotionally charged issue. It is possible to have fun and yet still be sensitive. What doesn't help, however, is cynical mickey taking or continual wind-ups, which tend to undermine trust.

Some kinds of feedback prove more useful than others. The main criteria for judging whether feedback is effective are whether it is useful to the other person, and whether they can develop as a result of hearing it. So much depends on how the information is delivered.

In an aligned team, the climate of support makes everyone more ready to talk about and tackle blocks to performance. There is less reticence and interchanges are remarkably frank and realistic. Difficulties seldom stay hidden for long.

Yet it takes hard work to establish an aligned team and difficulties are an essential part of its natural development cycle. Reaching alignment can involve uncomfortable periods during which people start to connect with each other, but they also compete, suffer from infighting and test the boundaries. This phase

> 'Why be difficult, when with a little extra effort you could be bloody impossible?'
> Card handed to actor Brenda de Banzie for her bitchiness on a film set

TEAM FEEDBACK

Actors rely on colleagues to help them develop their best performance. So there are often honest exchanges of feedback between cast members. Even if they don't interact much during the actual show, they might explore with a fellow actor ways to raise their performance to another level. In business you can establish coaching partnerships, so that people practise rehearsing with the support of a colleague.

You can use this pairing method further with teams in the workplace, by taking time out, perhaps an hour, on a regular basis. Members of the team sit opposite each other. The first team member has two minutes in which to tell the other person what they find most helpful and least helpful about their team behaviour. More specifically people say to each other: 'I want more of this' or 'I want less of that' or 'This is how I think you could add more value to my role'.

There is nothing tyrannical or confessional about this process! You don't have to say anything if you don't want to. Yet in practice people prove remarkably honest about how they experience each other and the exchanges are forthright and caring. After two minutes the two people reverse roles for a similar period and then everyone moves around to start another conversation with a new person.

This proves remarkably affirming to team relationships and undoubtedly strengthens the team's ongoing performance.

In working with business teams we sometimes encounter team leaders who are fearful of allowing such interchanges. They worry that perhaps the process will get out of control, people will worsen rather than improve their relationships with each other and so on. While such negative reactions are rare, they mainly arise because the team leader is inexperienced at handling conflict or relies on a divide-and-rule method for controlling the team.

If you are anxious about initiating the sort of frank feedback that the above approach generates, consider calling in a skilled team facilitator to get things moving. Once you have seen how people value the process and how relatively easy it is to steer safely, you will be hooked!

lets the group work towards alignment. However, some groups never progress further, becoming mired in a negative cycle of distrust and mutual antagonism.

One of the key purposes of formal team development is to help groups that are struggling with the alignment process confront reality and realize how much wasted time and energy go into maintaining the battle lines. That's why you sometimes might need to bring in an external facilitator.

External help can alter the status quo. Without some kind of formal development, dysfunctional teams may drift on without ever achieving alignment. They shelter behind a wall of operational busyness, or rely on the hierarchy to protect them from being called to account. Perhaps only when the company faces serious problems will the non-aligned group face a challenge to its way of working. There has to be a compelling reason for people to make the effort needed to form really productive relationships.

TAKE THAT!

TAKE 1: 'You're just rotten.'
Adds nothing, leaves me feeling bad.
TAKE 2: 'You're rotten when you behave like that.'
Still makes me feel bad. What exactly have I done wrong?
TAKE 3: 'I think you're rotten when you do that and you make me feel rotten.'
OK, so now I know I'm doing something wrong and what your reaction to it is.
TAKE 4: 'When you sneer at my ideas like that, you make me feel rotten.'
So it's sneering at your ideas that makes you feel bad.
TAKE 5: 'When you scoff at my ideas in a team meeting, I feel rotten because it shows me up in front of the others.'
I see, it's denigrating your ideas in front of the team that makes you feel bad.
TAKE 6: 'I hate it when you scoff at my ideas in a team meeting. I want you to treat my contribution with respect.'
Very specific. I understand it and realize what I have to do instead.

Go in the same direction

Many teams seem confused about their purpose or have simply 'lost the plot'. They may meet regularly and be engaged on a project together, yet there are few signs of the sort of cohesion and alignment that go beyond merely competent performance. The first place to look for the source of the problem is at the team's organization.

A crucial part of the team process in theatrical enterprises is that actors work to tight organizational and time boundaries. There are extremely short deadlines along with the essential planning and order. An aligned business team organizes itself like this too. That is, people seem clear about who does what and about their priorities. It is no good, for example, being a highly creative group if you are so inefficient that it sparks frustration and apathy.

You can recognize an incisively organized team from its daily operations, such as how it uses resources or its members' time. There are firm timescales that are treated as immutable. 'Chunking' (see page 84) also implies incisive organization. For example, does the team always break important aims into smaller parts, each with its own deadline for action?

Know what role you're all playing

Beryl, Errol and Darrell are discussing a stock-control problem with their supervisor.

SUPERVISOR: We keep running out of stock. What's the problem?
DARRELL: Beryl's the problem.
BERYL: Thanks, Darrell. Actually, I think you'll find it's Errol.
ERROL: Don't blame me. I always get blamed.
BERYL: Well, there's no one else to pick on, Errol.
ERROL: Great, you're scraping the bottom of the barrel, Beryl.

> BERYL: Is that meant to be a joke? Your humour goes so far over my head it's a danger to low-flying aircraft.
>
> DARRELL: You're in mighty peril, Errol.
>
> ERROL: Ha, ha.
>
> SUPERVISOR: Look, it's no good you all blaming each other. We've got to get to the bottom of this and work together. You're meant to be a team. You depend on each other to run this efficiently. When Darrell signs stuff out, Beryl needs to record it on the stock forms and Errol's meant to reorder. It's not rocket science.
>
> BERYL: I thought it was Darrell who records it when he signs it out.
>
> ERROL: No, I record it, but I thought Beryl was meant to sign it off.
>
> DARRELL: I didn't know I had to do anything! You're the supervisor. I thought you did it all.

It is essential to have clarity of roles and expectations in a team. Of course, in emergencies people may well pick up each other's roles just to get the job done. But on the whole, clear definitions and job descriptions work best. Paradoxically, the clearer you are about roles, the more freedom it gives you to break out of them and perhaps support a colleague and explore their activity. That can only happen when there are tight boundaries.

One of the most persistent myths about what happens in the performing arts is that it is undisciplined and rather 'flaky'. In fact, the best theatre, for example, results from incredible discipline. Not only does everyone involved need to know exactly what they're doing and be aligned to a common direction, but they also require shrewd organization. You can see this clearly in the making of major movies, where multimillion-dollar budgets are quickly squandered if they aren't carefully controlled. So storyboarding, shooting schedules and planning in minute detail become a way of life.

One crucial factor that allows this to work in the theatre is the structure of immutable deadlines. From the first meeting of the

--·--

PRODUCTION DEADLINES

It is hard for a team to perform outstandingly if there is no beginning or end to their activity. One idea is to turn ongoing activity into a project that has fixed stages or phases. Chunking up the process in this way not only allows for an injection of new energy at the start of each phase or a celebration at the end, but it helps with organization.

The stages of a theatrical production will include:

★   First meeting of production and performance team.
★   First read-through of the script.
★   First rehearsal.
★   First run-through of each act of the play.
★   First run-through of the whole play.
★   Technical rehearsal.
★   Dress rehearsal.
★   First preview.
★   Press night/opening night.
★   Last night.

What deadlines could you set that would focus people's efforts and help break the workload up into manageable phases?

--·--

team and the read-through right up to the opening night, there are milestones to mark performance deadlines. It keeps everyone on their toes.

Get behind the leader

Another prime requirement of a successful team is that people align around its leadership. This need not necessarily be just one person, although this tends to be the norm. Several people can in effect lead the team, depending on the tasks and challenges it faces.

The essence of aligned leadership is a clear sense of direction, one that fires people's imagination (more of that in Act III). Everyone needs to be enrolled in a common vision and encouraged to contribute fully in their own special way. If an outsider asked your team members to explain the team's main purpose or vision and their part in it, could they?

It is crucial that everyone in the team owns the vision. That means the leader guides the process, but remains receptive to the team members' input. You see this in the theatre when an entire cast knows what they are trying to achieve. Ask any of them about the purpose, concept or style of the production and you will probably receive a fulsome and consistent answer. That will be because they have been actively involved in interpreting the vision and contributing new ideas to bring it to fruition. After all, a play is simply words on a page. The team's job is to turn it into a dramatic performance. That involves everyone working closely with the leader.

Another sign of aligned leadership is that everyone subscribes to a common set of values that support the team's broader vision. The group continually tries to uncover practical solutions for converting vision and values into performance. If the team is involved in this process, it is easier for its members to support the leader. This is not about uncritical, blind allegiance; it is about pragmatic support in order to get the job done.

Sometimes different people may take the lead for particular purposes, but their leadership usually stays within a definite time boundary. Aligned leadership allows people to express themselves to the full because the boundaries are clear: they know how to contribute their unique talents while still feeling part of a tightly knit group.

The same can apply in your own 'theatre of work'. By creating a fixed term of leadership for a project or period, clarifying everyone's roles within the enterprise, and agreeing how you are

FIXED-TERM LEADERSHIP

One key characteristic of theatre teams is that they waste little time on leadership disputes, mainly because they are short term in nature. One of the benefits of a clearly defined end to a project is that people know they don't have to support the leader for ever.

Projects often fail because dissatisfaction with the leader breeds mutinous energy and performance is undermined. One of the benefits of the chunking process mentioned earlier, which converts long-term endeavours into short timeframes, is that it provides a chance for the leadership to be assessed and possibly changed at the end of the fixed term. It is much easier to back a leader completely when you know that you are operating within a fixed timeframe.

going to work together, you allow team members to back the leader. Alignment enables you to set off in the same direction.

Lead the team yourself

> 'I might have an idea of my own but I'm also trying to get great ideas out of my actors. If you have a strong vision, then you're able to throw it away for a better one.'
> Julie Taymor,
> director/playmaker

The Ambache is an orchestra that functions without a conductor. There may be a lead violinist and a soloist, but the orchestra produces exceptional performances, often with over 30 musicians, working as an ensemble. The same goes for many acting groups that work without a director. The performers take turns at stepping out of the action to provide an outside eye and give direction, but they dispense with the conventional authority figure.

Self-managed teams can be extremely demanding and are not an easy option for companies wanting dramatic performance. While they are not often used, research shows that they can be extremely productive.

The 'self-led' label can also be quite misleading. It does not mean that these teams should be leaderless. They usually benefit from designating one of their members to speak on behalf of the team and potentially resolve conflicts and issues around coordination and communication. However, leadership in such teams definitely moves around, depending on the situation.

Being self-led may mean that you will need to give up some of your conventional power. Nevertheless, you will know that the most effective leadership rests with those who have the most knowledge and expertise regarding a particular task. If you choose to take this option, remember the essential elements that have already been outlined: clear communication, continuous feedback and ongoing assessment of performance.

Self-led teams can be 15–20 per cent more productive than conventional teams, but it can take far more effort to develop them into star performers.

SCENE 2
TEAM CREATIVITY

Once a team is aligned, it can get on with its real purpose: to create, actually to produce or deliver something. A team ought to be able to create more than the sum of its parts, which is one of the reasons for its existence.

Actors share a ghastly anxiety dream, which goes something like this. They arrive late one night at a theatre without a script, don't know their lines and have forgotten to rehearse. The nightmare ends with finding themselves naked on stage in front of an expectant audience. Many business people have an equivalent dream. Their work environment feels like a play where the scenery keeps changing, the actors keep swapping roles and the script keeps being rewritten as they go along. In the managerial nightmare they don't know what the drama is about, where the plot is going or who the central characters are; while they believe that someone behind the scenes knows what's going on, they secretly fear that nobody does.

Today's teams face continual and often disruptive change. They are closer to chaos than appearances perhaps suggest. Consequently they have been called 'complex adaptive systems', responding almost organically to the uncertainties of their environment. In such a climate teams have to be adept at making things up as they go along.

In a changing environment you need to be a great improviser. This may seem the sort of talent that only great jazz musicians or comics possess, but it is familiar in our everyday lives. Our daily conversations are mainly spontaneous, we deal with local traffic conditions with hardly a second thought, and we improvise our way around the dance floor.

Each individual, as well as the team as a whole, needs to contribute creatively. We often get asked to help teams become more

'I just drive along in the car, talking to myself – improvising. People used to think, Uh-oh, loony in the car – now I just pretend I'm on the mobile phone.' Tracey Ullman, actor, on creating her characters

MORE FLEXIBILITY

To improvise successfully you need to be flexible. Once you get set in your ways your creativity is curtailed. No audience wants to watch actors simply going through the motions.

How do you become more flexible? A good start is simply to identify habits – and systematically to break them. Habits might include smoking, drinking, needing order, music, reading, sex, control, rebelliousness, over-eating, shopping, whatever. For instance, why bother reading newspapers and journals that agree with your thinking when you already know what you believe? Why not deliberately seek ideas that contradict your opinions with other viewpoints? In short, challenge your status quo! Get used to working with the unusual.

creative. We approach this task from the simple position that all human beings are naturally creative. You've only got to watch a group of children at play to see how spontaneously inventive they are. Everyone has obviously been a child, so the question is not 'What does it take to get people to be creative?' but really 'What is it that is stopping them being creative?'

There are two kinds of creativity killers: internal barriers and external ones. We are all creatures of habit. We may not be aware of it, but the way our brain functions is to create patterns that will make sense of the world. Thus we don't normally think new thoughts, merely replay old ones. Creativity demands that we think out of these 'boxes' that we live in. What drama-based approaches offer business is a way of encouraging you to act out of your box. By altering behaviour as well as thinking, you and your team stand a good chance of producing something exceptional.

External blocks to creativity include the rules, systems and procedures that stop us thinking or behaving afresh. An environment that rejects new ideas or suggestions, or where mistakes are not tolerated, is a tough one in which to create. So the first action

'Most people think two or three times a year. I have made an international reputation for myself by thinking once or twice a week.'
George Bernard Shaw, playwright

you can take to improve the creative output of your team is to go in search of anything that inhibits people's natural flair and inventiveness.

One of the first places to look is at your team meetings. Are they like creative playgrounds where the team is buzzing with energy and innovation? If not, read on…

Bring theatre to your meetings

While sports teams and orchestras play together and actors rehearse and perform together, most business teams don't function in this way. One of the main times they get together is in a meeting – yet we hear continual complaints of how much time is wasted in meetings. Most are seen as boring, ritualistic, stuck in procedure and generally rather pointless. Worse, they often inhibit people from giving their best.

What would it be like to work in a company where people actively look forward to their meetings, because they see them as exciting, productive and a wonderful chance to work creatively with their colleagues? It takes very little to transform meetings into occasions where participants do just that – participate.

To achieve this, you may need to start viewing meetings slightly differently, more like a theatre rehearsal than a procedural necessity. To start making them special, try adopting a stage director's approach. Think about each moment of the drama. What will make it compelling? What will engage the audience? What is the dynamic purpose of each section of the event? How can you remove the boring moments? What will keep it alive?

While many business teams manage to be fairly aligned and certainly well organized, they sometimes don't go beyond that. What's the point, if the team isn't going to strive for the very action that makes it more than the sum of its parts? It is the potential creativity of teams that makes them special.

'Never go to any meeting at the BBC. If you have to go to a meeting, stand, never sit. And always stand by the door so you can slip out with nobody noticing.'
John Humphrys, broadcaster

DRAMATIC MEETINGS

There are many techniques you can use to improve the drama of meetings. Here are just a few:

★ Change the scenery – hold the meeting in an unusual environment.
★ Vary the set – change the seating and room layout.
★ Have presentations.
★ Use props to demonstrate issues.
★ Have a flip chart so that people get up to use it and there is more energy.
★ Use storyboards for the agenda.
★ Call the audience to their seats.
★ Rotate the chair's role among team members.
★ Curtain up and down – always start and finish on time, to the minute.
★ Be action focused.
★ Make sure somebody owns every action. Cast people for the role.
★ Change the style and format each time.
★ Use double acts – get pairs of members to prepare an input to the group.
★ Always incorporate a creative process.
★ Use the meeting as an opportunity to find out more about each other.

A team can only produce outstanding performance if everyone contributes. Meetings are a good place for this to happen, but sometimes we hear leaders complain that their team members don't speak up or make much of an input. Why? Often it is because the leader is impatient, over-controlling and wanting to direct exactly what happens.

THE CONTROLLING TEAM LEADER'S DIARY

Today: There's no time wasting at my team meetings. We get through the business efficiently and on time.

One month later: I've had a direction from on high. Seems they want to encourage involvement among the staff. They recommend I seek suggestions and ideas from my team. Fair enough. Can't think they'll have much to say, but I'll give it a go next time.

Next month: Ran a team meeting today. Followed instructions and asked for ideas, suggestions and comments from the team. Surprise, surprise. Nobody said a word. Typical. You give people a chance and they've got nothing to say. I suppose that's why I'm the leader. Back to normal at the next team meeting as far as I'm concerned.

While the above may be a slight exaggeration, we frequently encounter team leaders who have little understanding of what it takes to get people really talking, contributing and being creative.

There are plenty of ways in which you can begin to promote a better team response than the above approach. These can be quite challenging if you insist on trying to run such a tight ship that people feel there is no real room for them to make a creative contribution. However, by making people other than the chair responsible for sections of the meeting, you can encourage everyone to have a voice. That also allows you to step back a little and contribute in a different way.

To promote a discussion about comedy and what quality comedy truly means, BBC director general Greg Dyke called his top team to a meeting and instead of lecturing them on the finer points of script writing, insisted that they all watched his favourite programme: *The Office*. Message received.

GET EVERYONE INVOLVED

As with many theatre productions, the Royal Shakespeare Company's rehearsals for *Nicholas Nickleby* involved everyone in research projects. Over a lengthy period of collaboration, the co-directors John Caird and Trevor Nunn asked members of the cast to take responsibility for bringing in background material on aspects of the piece. Two actors researched and presented a talk with slides about the early Victorian theatre. Others studied the class system, education, medicine and hygiene – anything that might prove relevant. The more the actors got involved in the research process, the more they made huge personal investments in the show. Because it was an ensemble production, with the actors playing a variety of roles, casting was not complete until everyone had played many roles during rehearsal. So the cast saw beyond merely their own part and started feeling responsible for the production as a whole.

Involving people in this way invites investment. Giving people responsibilities encourages them to make personal commitments to aspects of a project. And making people temporary experts gives them a personal connection, as well as providing a development opportunity.

In your own 'rehearsals' you can encourage involvement by asking different team members to prepare something in advance or to lead sections of the meeting. You could hold time-limited brainstorming sessions in order to throw ideas around and get everyone's views. You could get people working in pairs, asking them to tell a story or giving them a role in which they have to elicit material from other people, and so on. You might not get much of a response right away, as these things take time. Yet after a while, when team members see that they can have an influence on proceedings, they are likely to be bursting with ideas.

Experiment!

When there is an atmosphere of freedom to experiment, where ideas are thrown around and things tried out, it generates a buzz of concentrated energy. Meetings can be exciting. As stage director Richard Eyre says, 'Rehearsals are a time when actors can experiment, invent, explore, discuss, dispute, practise and become child-like, and it is the job of the director to create a world – private and secure – where this activity can go on without fear of failure.'

When the team works together, whether in a meeting or in daily activity, this is always an opportunity to be creative. It is where the natural ability to improvise comes in. Successful improvisation depends entirely on each person being willing to accept others' ideas and build on them. Accept and build is the improviser's mantra. In practice this means saying 'yes' to ideas and then trying to enhance or add value to them.

> 'I want people to be desperate to get out of bed and come to rehearsal.'
> Stephen Berkoff, director

Trust the power of yes

Listen out for the language used most frequently in your own team. For instance, which word pops up most often: yes, no or but? Do people also build on each other's ideas, rather than killing them off with muted enthusiasm or negative criticism?

'Yes, but...' is a phrase that comes from a negative world that is fearful and forces unnecessary choices. It views things as fixed dualities. In contrast, 'Yes, and...' assumes creative potential, where alternatives, contradictions and paradoxes are embraced because they are often the source and stimulus of invention.

If you can hear another team member's contribution as an offering that might allow you to create something of value, then you remove the impulse to kill it off. You can accept it for what it is without having to criticize it, and just build on it. See if you can say 'yes' to ideas and comments made by colleagues and create new

> 'If you obey all the rules you miss all the fun.'
> Katharine Hepburn, actor

TIPS TO ENCOURAGE EXPERIMENTATION

How do you stimulate your own creativity as a way of improving your ability to improvise?

★   Seek outside stimuli – visit other companies and see how they work. Make sure that some of those you visit are completely different to your own. For example, churches, concert halls, retirement homes, racetracks, funfairs, coal mines, theatres, hospitals and shopping centres – anywhere you can spot creativity being applied in a completely different way to that in your own company. Then see if there's anything at all you could learn from what those companies do.

★   Work closely with creative people, rather than delegating this role to others.

★   Look for strange and unexpected connections between what you do and what is around you.

★   Set yourself some creative personal challenges – for example, to have one entirely new experience every month.

★   Entertain the possibility that nothing you believe in is necessarily true. See where such thinking leads you.

★   Devise creative problem-solving situations with friends and colleagues.

★   Change how you take notes – try mind mapping to avoid linear thinking, or use storyboards with pictures.

★   Conduct thought experiments that use 'What if?' scenarios.

★   Locate the mavericks in your organization and spend time regularly listening to them.

YES!

Most improvisation depends on saying 'yes' to any idea that someone throws at you. Rather than judging or qualifying it in any way, you simply go with the idea, seeing where it takes you.

Start by exploring the difference between 'Yes, but...' and 'Yes, and...' to experience the varying energy of each statement. For instance, with a partner spend a few moments when one of you suggests ideas for, say, a marketing event or Christmas party. The other person responds to every suggestion with 'Yes, but that's no good because...' Now try it where one person suggests how you might spend a day or evening out, and the response is 'Yes, and we could then do/go...' Each person builds on the other's idea. Give it a minute or two and see where you end up.

You could move on to more sophisticated improvisations, generating extraordinary ideas in a spirit of spontaneity and play. You might create a story by contributing one word at a time, starting with 'once', 'upon', 'a' and 'time'.

Many other exercises take the same principle and sometimes unusual solutions and commercial innovations emerge from the process. All are triggered from simply saying 'yes'. Anything can happen, and often does.

ideas with them. In that way you value their input and see it as an opportunity. And it is more likely that you will then invent something quite unexpected.

Some managers are afraid that if they immediately respond positively to people's ideas things will get rapidly out of hand. They worry that absurd projects might start exploding across the business. This is most unlikely, since the 'yes' device is only the start of a feasibility exercise to reveal whether an idea is useful or not. The main purpose of the method is to avoid killing off a potentially brilliant idea at birth. We are not advocating blind, unquestioning obedience, merely positive exploration.

The most common idea-generation exercise used in business is brainstorming. Its purpose is to get ideas that wouldn't normally emerge if conventional thinking were pursued. The team is asked to think the unthinkable. However, the process is often conducted in a solemn and downbeat way – hardly an encouragement to yield wild ideas. Worse still, there is an over-dependence on brainstorming as if it were the only way to get people playing with ideas.

It is no coincidence that the word used to describe a drama is 'play'. If you can create a playful environment you are more likely to generate a team atmosphere that fosters and values creativity and improvisation. Many companies do their best to generate humour and fun at work. Having a good time does not detract from people's commitment and application. For example, some of the most resolute and engaged activity happens when companies start generating money for charities such as Comic Relief. People can work hard and still have a lot of fun doing it.

Use the whole person

If creative potential is locked away within team members, you need to release it to get more out of the team. ACE teams – those that are aligned, creative and exploring – exhibit professional know-how

> 'I think fun should be a motivator for all business. We've been successful because we've done things differently and that's made life more fun and enjoyable.'
> Richard Branson, entrepreneur

> '90% of this wild exploration was useless. But 10% took me to places I would never have dreamed of.'
> Paul Newman, actor

TEAM CASTING

How do you cast your team members?

Within a team it can often be worth examining to what extent the team has labelled certain members and restricted their full potential, preventing them from using all of themselves.

For example, a team may label its finance person a hard-nosed realist, when in fact this person may have many other under-used qualities that could benefit team performance.

Of course, it takes imagination and a flexible approach to tap into a person's ability to contribute in what are perhaps unusual ways. For example, who on the team loves organizing parties and celebrations? Which team member uses intuition superbly when it comes to recruiting new people? Is there someone who naturally re-energizes the team when people are feeling jaded?

You could use performance reviews as an occasion for each team member to commit to doing something new, something innovative, for the team.

'Have you ever seen a man sit down at the piano and play the same note over and over again? If you see a great concert pianist, they use all the notes, all the colours, all the graduations.'
Preston Sturges,
director

and specific skills while fully engaging every aspect of the person – their physicality, intellect, emotions and intuition – in a balanced, healthy way.

One of the joys of acting is that it uses so many of these aspects of a person. The text demands intellect, the character's feelings require empathy, the creative process asks for intuitive innovation, and the whole experience of performing uses the actor's energy – physical, sexual and psychic. A theatrical performance can feel like a thorough work-out in all these areas, which is why it is often so exhausting.

How can your business team encourage people to give of themselves fully – their enthusiasm, creativity, talents and potential? Often team preferences push people into typecast roles, when the people themselves might have wider capabilities. This tendency to typecast both actors and individual team members wastes potential. It could be useful to explore this as an item on a team meeting agenda. Take ten minutes to create ways in which each person could bring their total self to the team's enterprise. Such a discussion could highlight areas where people feel restricted or unfulfilled.

Be curious

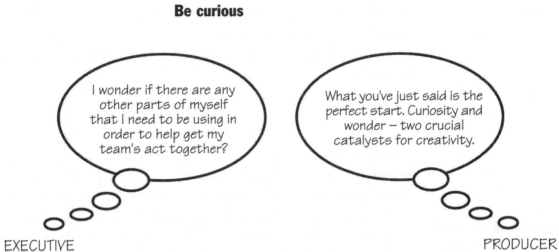

I wonder if there are any other parts of myself that I need to be using in order to help get my team's act together?

What you've just said is the perfect start. Curiosity and wonder – two crucial catalysts for creativity.

EXECUTIVE   PRODUCER

Curiosity acts as a springboard to creativity. Immersed in daily judgements and decisions, team members can often under-value the importance of simply being curious. 'It is not easy to be curious,' says Durk Jager, ex-CEO of healthcare giant Procter & Gamble. 'The external environment might favour it, but the culture within most companies does not. Generally, we reward certainty. And we look askance at uncertainty, much less outright confusion. But you have to persevere in the face of such resistance. The pursuit of certainty leads you to a narrow view of the world, and it slows you down in ways no business can afford.'

Jager, like creative artists and inventors, knows that the creative process often starts with a question: 'What would happen if...?' It is impossible to think afresh or create something new when we approach it from a fixed view of the world. 'My comfort with not understanding and my passion for figuring it out is the one thing, more than any other, that enables me to lead in a world for which there is no preparation,' says Jager. 'So get curious. Figure it out. And enjoy the process that gets you there.'

The improvised drama of today's workplace demands new skills. If we become mired in judgements, expectations, assumptions and fixed ways of behaving, we will find it hard to survive, let alone thrive. The healthier option is to bring our curiosity to situations, try to make sense of them, and then see what we can create as a result.

Wonder

The other great source of team creativity is wonder. The famous 'What if?' question mentioned earlier has led to innumerable inventions. Fred Smith, founder of Federal Express, wondered why there couldn't be a reliable overnight mail service. Masaru Ibuka of Sony wondered what would happen if the company removed the recording function and speakers from a cassette machine and used headphones, thus creating the Walkman. Trevor Baylis, inventor of Freeplay, the clockwork radio, wondered why poor people in underdeveloped countries had to keep buying expensive batteries to power the sound. James Dyson wondered if vacuum cleaners had to have endless replacement bags and lose their suction.

Very young children seem continually surprised, constantly in a state of wonder. Watch the awe on an infant's face when they encounter something new or unexpected. Yet we can lose this sense of wonder as we age, often replacing it with cynicism. What if we pause and really look? How can we not be in total wonder when we contemplate the structure of a sunflower, migrating swallows, microchip technology, seahorses, the way mould forms on a decaying peach, conception, the Lascaux cave paintings, the taste of

'Humanity never moves forward as a result of asking pertinent questions – only by asking impertinent questions.'
Alan Plater, playwright

'Imagination, industry and intelligence – "the three Is" – are all indispensable to the actress but, of these three, the greatest is, without doubt, imagination.'
Ellen Terry, actor

tears, spontaneous combustion, the endless varieties of orchid, DNA testing, chameleons, an aeroplane taking off, the Sistine Chapel, the way blood congeals, Stonehenge, spiders' webs or the myriad stars above us? (That's the start of our list – what's yours?)

What stops us bringing that same sense of wonder and curiosity to the drama unfolding in our own organizations? Most of what happens will be a mystery. You cannot guarantee what will happen in your team. By all means lay down the best plans possible and set all the right processes going, but then you will just have to wait and wonder what will happen. 'Nobody knows anything,' as William Goldman memorably commented about the ability of Hollywood to predict what would be a successful movie. And as the saying goes, 'If you want to make God laugh, tell her your plans.'

That's why being childlike can be so important. Notice that we mean childlike, not childish. Seeing through the eyes of a child can be a great source of innovation. And teams, by playing together, can support each other in bringing a freshness of approach to any situation.

> 'It's the innocence of childhood, when we were still open, when we could still paint a tree and let it look any way we liked, the time before somebody came up and said: "A tree looks like this and you must paint it so."'
> Liv Ullmann, actor

TIME TO WONDER

People need 'wondering time'. This should be booked into diaries, individually and collectively. It can be some of the most valuable time ever spent. A report from the Roffey Park Management Institute on how directors think found that the best ideas occur away from the workplace – commonly when people are on their own and in relaxed settings, such as on train or plane journeys, walking the dog or on the beach. Teams, as well as individuals, need 'reflective time' for creativity to gestate.

Expect trials and tribulations

Creative teamworking can be a frustrating activity. If only we could predict creativity. It would be so convenient simply to program it into the diary: 'Innovative breakthrough, next Tuesday, 11.05 am.' Of course, it never happens like that.

The creative process is a rollercoaster, alternating between struggle, hope, despair, excitement, frustration, fear, expectation, sweat, ecstasy, disappointment, relief and a whole lot more. This scary journey can take a few moments or maybe years. You can't predict or legislate for invention – only stimulate, support and allow for it. Knowing that this is the common experience of creative teams at least allows you to weather the storm, deal with the anxiety and get on with the work in hand.

When people use all of themselves in the creative team process, they become so fully engaged that they may have fewer inhibitions about expressing their feelings. This can take its toll in even the best-organized team and consequently there need to be opportunities for people to let off steam. Temperament can be a source of team energy.

'If we don't get lost we'll never find a new route.'
Joan Littlewood, director

SCENE 3
TEAM EXPLORATION

In the 1930s a Russian theatre company rehearsed Nikolai Erdman's play *Suicide* for 18 months. The authorities attending the dress rehearsal then banned the production for its 'subversive' views. The play was never publicly performed in the USSR, and it wasn't until 1979 that it was performed at all – in the UK.

Erdman's experience shows that it is not enough to create a great ensemble company, where rehearsals are fantastic and the production has all the promise of success. Ultimately, the team – aligned and creative though it may be – has to get out there and perform.

Exploration is the third essential element required to become an ACE team. An exploring team looks to make its impact in the internal or external marketplace and brings back to the enterprise fresh thinking and stimulus.

> 'Acting, however beautiful a craft it is for oneself, has finally got to be for them – the audience.'
> Ralph Richardson, actor

Be adventurous

Peter Brook's experimental theatre company based in France devised a production around the great mythic tale *Mahabharata*. It opened in Paris and then toured internationally, performing the piece to some of the world's most 'primitive' tribes. Closer to home, Glen Walford set up the London Bubble in the 1970s to take theatre to people in communities who would not normally set foot in a conventional playhouse. The company toured in a tent, giving its performances the accessibility of circus. And when community theatre became a fully fledged concept, theatre productions saw no boundaries, showing up in museums, narrow boats, parks, factories and even on the London Underground.

Developing a spirit of adventure in your team means making it a priority to help both the individual members and the team as a

> 'Some nights they're porridge; some nights electricity.'
> Sybil Thorndike, actor, on audiences

For your team to perform outstandingly you will need to break the mould, find your own unique style and, where necessary, go beyond your current confines to make an impact.

You mean exploring new territories, seeking fresh markets, and forging new links with different sorts of customers. My team doesn't deal directly with external customers, but there's no reason why the same approach won't work inside the organization.

PRODUCER

EXECUTIVE

whole take risks and avoid playing safe. And these risks aren't necessarily purely business ones. Sometimes risk is merely trusting a team member with a difficult or essential task, stretching them beyond their normal capabilities, or the entire team taking on an audacious project.

It is also a matter of using supportive relationships within the team to build outside relationships, sharing the group's values and building a profile. While enriching your team, it equally enriches those with whom the team comes into contact. People detect a group whose members are focused and channelled. They rapidly realize that this team is special. Many small companies manage to win large contracts from mega-corporations simply by showing that they are ACE teams, providing outstanding performance.

Being adventurous doesn't mean abandoning your strengths in order to explore new territories. Often it is a question of adapting or building on what your team already does well, but extending it into new areas. Aardman Animations, for instance, started with plasticine characters on children's television. The company then used its skill and unique talent for commercials, before making the Oscar-winning *Wallace and Gromit* trilogy of short films. This led to

CONNECTING WITH CUSTOMERS

For those focusing on client and customer relations, drama-based development can offer some useful ideas. Techniques that actors use when building a character can be applied to understanding customers. Recall the questions posed in Act I Scene 3 (Know your colleagues better, page 53) and adapt them to finding out more about your customers. Then look at how these clients could be treated in order to provide star service.

Improvising customer interactions can be a great way of troubleshooting problems. By freeze-framing the scene occasionally and allowing other 'actors' to continue with their own solutions, you produce options for dealing with difficulties.

When it comes to building client relations, you can use the storyline of a deepening relationship to inform your approach. It's not quite as crude as 'boy meets girl', but you can look at each of the elements of starting as strangers; attracting; making contact; flirting; first date; courting; trusting; loyal friend; and finally marriage or partnership. Explore the nature of the relationship and what will allow it to deepen.

opportunities in the feature film market and the funding to make the full-length movie *Chicken Run*. It can be just as revolutionary to be evolutionary.

Add value

Actors performing in a long-running show are continually 'raising the bar', always seeking improvements. It's one of the ways they stay fresh and interested. The managerial equivalent is *kaizen* or continuous improvement. It is quite common for a stage director to revisit a production, having left it to run for a while, and be staggered by the changes the cast and crew have made.

How can you continually add value to your organization? It could be through your decisions, contacts, knowledge, experience, relationships and so on. There may be no single route, since

> 'Stamina is everything. Stamina, balls and confidence. You've got to just keep going.'
> Whoopi Goldberg, performer

VALUE-ADDED INITIATIVES

At Hewlett-Packard we ran a series of workshops, many with intact teams, to generate ideas for adding value to the business. People kept producing initiatives that would improve performance and add commercial value. They were asked to focus on ideas that they could implement themselves, rather than coming up with a list of actions that other people needed to do. What mattered beyond the list of great ideas, however, was how HP's leadership reacted to this outpouring.

MD Phil Lawler and HR director Kate Patton signalled how important these contributions were by making themselves available weekly for presentations from those attending the workshops. Though the emphasis was on what the participants could make happen themselves, it was important that senior leadership was receptive.

In contrast, another client of ours in the financial sector, pursuing a similar programme, sent a directive saying: 'Please don't encourage too many ideas, as the board has too long a list already.'

> 'If new ideas are constantly turned down, it turns people off, they stop generating ideas no matter how much you pay them.'
> Anita Roddick,
> The Body Shop

companies are now too complex and fast moving for any one person to control. Adding value therefore starts within your team. To produce more than the sum of the parts, each member must somehow add value to the others.

It's your front-line performers who can spot improvements to themselves, their office, their environment, their customer service and their processes. To take advantage of their knowledge and willingness to contribute, you need to promote a team culture that welcomes, collects and applies their contributions.

Use theatre as a sales tool

While show business uses many of the conventional sales methods, from billboards to advertising campaigns, it is particularly good at creating experiences. This offers important resources for the world of business, particularly in the area of selling.

Selling through providing experiences leads to some novel methods that are often fun and fast and can lead to dramatic sales results. Here are some of the ways in which theatre can help.

Create experiences

Customers for products and services increasingly want more than merely being sold something. Instead, they demand an experience that excites them in some way. So Selfridges' successful transformation of its Oxford Street store in London came about because its managers viewed shopping as not just selling goods but providing an environment where customers could taste a different lifestyle. The result was a decision to place coffee shops and themed snack bars among the designer clothes.

This is what theatre is all about, creating new and exciting kinds of customer experiences. Traditionally this used to mean offering a powerful dramatic experience on stage. More recently, though, theatre has gone further, producing a total environmental extravaganza where the audience becomes part of the action. For example, by the end of the legendary Blue Man Group show, now performing in Boston, New York and Las Vegas, the audience is part of a frenzy of mountains of paper and music, rocking with laughter and delight.

For today's companies and industrial enterprises, the new challenge is increasingly to promote what they sell using similar methods.

Work as a team

'Sales teams' can often be a contradiction in terms. Most sales operations seem anything but a team. They usually consist instead of a

PROVIDE AN EXPERIENCE

Parading in the streets in full costume and make-up is merely one way in which the theatre business tries to give its potential customers a sense of what the show will be like. The Edinburgh Festival provides a lively example of this, when walking the streets for half an hour gives an instant taste of many of the shows in town.

Sharing customers' reactions to what you offer also provides invaluable endorsements. In the theatre that means quoting what the critics say and hearing what the audience thinks about the performance. Vox pop interviews with audience members as they leave the theatre capture how people feel about the event, or better still there are pictures of people laughing or crying in the aisles. This all conveys the emotional reaction of satisfied customers. This approach works just as well with all kinds of experiential products.

A theatrical approach applied to selling uses creativity to provide customer experiences. Instead of talking about benefits, you invent interesting and exciting ways to give people a taste of the product or service in action. For example, showcases, taster sessions, trial periods and free seminars prompt people to respond in a visceral way to the product.

group of individuals who are rewarded on how they outperform each other, rather than collaborating. They chase individual targets, hoard leads and client relationships, and vie with each other to be sales person of the year.

Yet increasingly selling demands a team effort, particularly with complex sales. In the acting world, whatever the personal rivalries, on stage the star of the show can only shine if the rest of the cast provides the right kind of support. The theatrical team methods explored in this book can enliven and transform teams, prompting individuals to alter their attitude to each other in the search of collective as well as individual success.

Thus, instead of hitting the phones in a relentless epidemic of cold calling (or 'pestering', as it is more aptly named) the team members work together creatively on key account or client activity. They pool their knowledge from their different interactions with clients and customers. They support each other to devise imaginative ways of promoting their wares.

Rewarding overall performance with a team bonus, rather than individually, can be a great incentive and support to this way of working.

Be authentic

Actors learn to embody what they sell, since they are constantly attending auditions where they are closely scrutinised. They may be asked to perform a short piece or read a section of the script, and their performances may be videotaped. In such a cattle market, they can only succeed by coming across as authentic.

Much the same applies increasingly in other spheres of customer-facing activity. So much now depends on being able to establish trust. Customers quickly detect manipulation and jaded sales techniques. In its crudest form, for instance, if you sell a product that you say is high quality, then that is how you must come across. The most effective sales people are therefore authentic. They are clearly telling the truth and present their products with an obvious sense of commitment and honest admiration. They are often genuinely excited about the product or service on offer, and it shows.

> 'What I try to do is make things as clear and as authentic as possible.'
> Robert de Niro, actor

Keep the script fresh

Some forms of selling rely on using a tightly controlled script, to which you as a sales person must stick closely or risk censure. But continual repetitions of the script can soon produce a stilted, unconvincing result.

Actors must stick to the script as well, repeating it night after night. So they learn to find a personal connection with the material

109

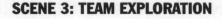

AUTHENTIC SELLING

The most successful sales people have a glow or sparkle around them. They don't have to work hard at selling the product. There's something about them as human beings that attracts customers.

In working with sales people who seem to have lost this ability, we conduct what might be called anti-sales training. This involves using the actor's approach of gaining connection.

Actors need to connect with their character; for sales people it's about finding a connection with their product. That is why our presentation courses help people contact their passion for their subject so that they can speak with integrity and authenticity about it. As a participant once told us, 'I've spent years learning and trying to implement a whole host of sales techniques – everything from the opening to the closing of a sale. And loads of ways of manipulating the in-between. Now I realize the best technique is to just be myself.'

they have to present. This connection allows them to bring the script to life every time they deliver it. They find a way of using their own personality to reveal the script's message. By connecting with their enthusiasm, experience, warmth and concern, they make it more credible and add colour to it.

Another useful technique in preparing to deliver a script is rewriting it as you would like to speak it. That means breaking it up at every introduction of a new idea.

Actors will often write on scripts to help them think about delivery. They remind themselves of ideas or images they might use to convey the appropriate feeling. Working on a script in this way is all part of the rehearsal process.

This paragraph of the book
is presented as if it were a sales script
and laid out
as you might speak it.
Each new idea demands a new line and a new energy when delivering it.
This helps the presenter think about the ideas that have to be communicated
and ensures that they don't merely
reel off a load of meaningless words.
Yes, it ends up looking a little like a poem.
It is an expression of colloquial, rather than written speech.
Believe it or not,
this is the way Winston Churchill wrote his great speeches.

Build a relationship

Whether using a script or simply talking to customers, you need to adapt continually, thinking on your feet. This means showing that you are alert, alive and can really listen to build a trusting relationship. The ideas we presented on improvisation and presence earlier are obviously beneficial here. Another useful acting technique you can use to help nurture healthy sales relationships involves status.

As a sales person, you may need to talk convincingly to high-level individuals who will only take you seriously if you can somehow match their status. Likewise, there may be occasions when you meet sales prospects who regard themselves as particularly low status, and it would be unwise for you to behave with high status. Status does not depend on title or position; it is generally due to how you feel about yourself. In selling, it often pays to adjust your status to build trust.

By expanding your repertoire of expression, you open up new sales possibilities. To succeed at selling you need a wide range of

ADDING THEATRICAL VALUE TO CUSTOMERS

Complex organizations such as a supermarket operation look for an unending stream of creative ideas to enhance the shopping experience. When CEO Carlos Criado-Perez arrived at Safeway, he brought with him his concept of 'retailtainment' – a commitment to making shopping in a supermarket an enjoyable experience. This started with the 'Fresh To Go' team providing fresh take-away food. Teams were asked to look at everything from making sure that each area of the 'stage' is exciting to ensuring that customers/audience can be delighted with attentive service and an element of pizzazz.

The team needed to become star performers, showing warmth, positive energy, humour, sensitivity, listening, confidence, creativity, commitment and, most of all, genuineness. The sort of behaviour needed to add value was rather like being a good actor; that is, being truthful rather than fake. Using ideas from the theatre, teams were encouraged to find their own creative response to customer contacts. With sketches, improvisations and coaching, front-line staff explored the possibilities of good and bad customer service. They were encouraged to be creative, risky and have fun. Through this process people saw how to build and strengthen appropriate relationships.

The 25 members of the store management team threw themselves into the programme. If they were willing to 'shake out' and sing, then so could everyone else. 'You mean I can just be me?' marvelled one tough, rather diffident counter hand who, for the first time, felt he could find his own way to add value to the shopping experience for those he encountered.

External independent measures showed that customer service satisfaction shot up from 44 per cent in the summer of 2000, to 90 per cent after the training ended. The average score for similar stores in East London was 54 per cent. The success of the Fresh To Go team showed up in sales that rose from £21,000 per week when the store reopened to over £34,000 per week, with a continuing upward trend.

PRACTISE STATUS

You can experiment with the issue of status using a popular theatre improvisation.

Start thinking about status on a scale of 1–10. What would the various levels look and feel like? There are distinct behaviours, body language, feelings and thoughts attached to different statuses. For example, if you had a status of Level 1, how would you walk around, what would you say, how might you react to meeting someone at level 10?

On our workshops people enact a short scene – a meeting between two people – after choosing a non-picture playing card with a fixed status number on it. Depending on what card you draw, you alter your behaviour to indicate your status. People doing the exercise soon realise that status is more a state of mind than something reflecting their position in either society or a company. Such improvisations allow people to find ways of altering their own attachments to status and consequently interacting better with others.

methods and approaches on which to draw. If you can only perform as a pushy order seeker, for example, then you will almost certainly find many sales situations closed to you. Instead, you need more choices, more ways to tap into the different parts of your personality. The rewards will be enormous.

'Every crowd has a silver lining.'
PT Barnham, producer

Take risks

The show *Blood Brothers* is a good example of the sort of creative risks common in theatre and how they can contribute to dramatic performance. Despite a sell-out season at the Liverpool Playhouse, obtaining backing to stage the musical elsewhere proved troublesome. So the producers resorted to unusual methods on both sides of the Atlantic.

BILL KENWRIGHT (PRODUCER): It's never been a critic's show but it's always been an audience's show. When we opened in London we had the smallest advance of any musical ever to open in the West End and I just said, 'Listen, build it, and they will come.' We charged a fiver a ticket for the first two weeks and by week three you couldn't get in.

Eventually Blood Brothers transferred to Broadway, and on the opening night...

BILL KENWRIGHT: The ovation went for about 11 minutes – the biggest ever on Broadway. And I went to my advertising agent's office, which is what you do on Broadway. We switch on the radio and the reviews start.

CRITICS: '*Blood Brothers* is bloody awful.' 'Willy Russell wrote the music – Willy Russell gives me the willies.'

BILL KENWRIGHT: And it got worse and worse and worse. We got slaughtered. I came down to breakfast and obviously everyone said you'd better not talk to him, because he's just lost his house, his car, his shirt, everything. I had this wonderful treasurer called Herman Pearl and I said: 'What do you think?'

HERMAN PEARL: 'Take it off, take if off tonight. Reviews like those mean it's all over.'

BILL KENWRIGHT: 'I'll tell you what we'll do (there was a matinee on): if you and I walk in there at the end of the show and they don't stand I'll take it off. If they stand I'm staying on for the fight.' So the curtain comes down, nobody stands and Herman looks at me and I have a tear in my eye. Then, suddenly, one person stands, then another, then someone with a Zimmer frame and in the end they're all standing, screaming. It was known as the miracle of Broadway. I've produced it all over the world now. I think we must have done 10,000 performances and we truly have had 10,000 standing ovations.

Like Kenwright, to achieve outstanding rather than competent and predictable performance, your team will need to do things differently. That means stepping into the unknown. It is a huge risk and feels incredibly scary.

HOW RISKY IS YOUR TEAM?

★   Does your team encourage calculated risk taking?

★   Does your workplace look bold and different?

★   What has your team done that is bold and different?

★   Are you aware of the process the team goes through when it takes risks?

★   Do you review what you've learnt from any risks taken?

These are the sorts of questions you need to pose if you want to improve your team culture. An important ingredient of team performance is a readiness to take risks. And being aware of the process allows teams to learn from the outcomes – both successes and failures. This is how people learn and avoid making even worse mistakes. It's also important because it is only through risk taking that teams make extraordinary things happen.

Theatre companies take these risks all the time, leading to acclaim if they are successful or humiliation if they flop. The great aspect of teamworking, whether in the theatre or in business, is that you are not alone. Everyone shares the pain and the pleasure. There is mutual comfort in knowing you have your colleagues with you. It is another area of performance where there is strength in numbers.

And theatre ensembles minimize the risks by doing 'try-out' tours, where the piece is refined in the light of audience response. In this process plays are rewritten and reworked, and sometimes the production changes almost completely. Rehearsal becomes continuous development, with actors often learning new lines overnight for the next day's performance. What's important, though, is not so much the rehearsal or the preview, it's whether the team is learning from it. If they don't improve, it's a waste.

Research shows that generally teams take more risks than individuals! However, there is always a danger that riskiness

> 'You know that you are frightened. What makes you a professional is that you are used to being afraid. You accept fear.'
> Ralph Richardson, actor

LET'S DO THE SHOW RIGHT HERE, RIGHT NOW

You will take risks when you

★   leave your personal comfort zone;
★   act in a non-compliant way;
★   handle rejection, disagreement or failure.

While some people are naturally more able to tolerate risk than others, people generally show clear signs of being able to learn and practise some of these behaviours.

Try generating a theatrical environment in your team in which you 'put the show on right away'. In other words, adopt a 'do it now' culture. For example, when anyone has an idea, an impulse to do or create anything, adopt the driving motto of 'Let's do it right now', make it happen immediately. The whole focus is on generating action that could be taken at once.

Occasionally, if it proves impossible to take instant action, write it in the team's diaries, committing people to action. The important factor is to create an atmosphere where anything can happen – and it can happen right now.

'I've learnt from my mistakes and I'm sure I can repeat them.'
Peter Cook, humourist

becomes recklessness. It is a matter of judgement, and fortunately it is one of those equations that a team seems more able to calculate than an individual. Your team members can highlight the risks involved and whether they put your company's future in jeopardy. That is a good working definition of recklessness. If it commits you to expenditures for which there are inadequate funds or it severely damages your reputation with clients, then it may be a reckless folly rather than a legitimate risk. What is important is to make sure that people are kept fully informed about the implications of their actions.

Your willingness to take risks can be inspiring to those around you. James Dyson built a world-class company that overtook market leader Hoover by taking informed risks that enabled him to overcome frequent setbacks. When Phillips Plastics tried to hold him to ransom on the cost of assembling his innovative cleaner, he refused to be intimidated and took the risk of setting up alternative facilities elsewhere. His persistence, initiative and risk taking continue to attract a talented team of young designers to his company.

Phil Knight, founder and chairman of sports apparel company Nike, has argued that 'the trouble with America is not that we are making too many mistakes, but that we are making too few'. This was an astute observation, since it is impossible to strive for brilliant performance without taking risks. And taking risks means that you are bound not to get it right every time. Mistakes are part of the process. The only issue is whether your team can learn from them – as a CEO of 3M once put it, 'We can afford almost any mistake, once.'

Learning through making mistakes is how ACE teams grow and develop. It allows your team to harness its learning and continually improve its performance. For explorers, there is always discovery.

> 'Ever tried. Ever failed. No matter. Try again. Fail again. Fail better.'
> Samuel Beckett, playwright/director

Share learning

Shows transfer from the fringe to the mainstream, from arts festivals to Broadway or London's West End. For that to happen, learning has to occur. If it does, small successes can become major achievements. For instance, Michael Frayn's hit comedy *Noises Off* started as a one-act play before being expanded into a full-length farce. The musical *Blood Brothers* began as a play for young people, without music, and was first performed in a comprehensive school. The West End hit show *Return to the Forbidden Planet* was initially a late-night entertainment at the London Bubble Theatre.

Major products start as small seeds. Your team's job is to spot these opportunities, and that can only happen when you've created a learning environment.

While many business teams talk about knowledge management, they sometimes forget that it starts with individuals gaining the knowledge and then talking about it to others in the team. You could run separate team sessions about this, or have a regular agenda item where people report back on some research they've conducted or an area of best practice they've encountered.

There are no upper limits to team performance, in theatre or business. So the best teams continually use their own performance to learn how to improve still further. Such teams tend to be fascinated with feedback, whether negative or positive. It helps if you are hungry to know about the effect your team is having on people.

Managing change is a core part of any successful production. A long-running musical will change its cast every year, for example. These alterations are not made on a whim. They stem from the recognition that people are not robots. Performers become stale, situations alter, audiences change their views about who they want to see performing and so on.

In the case of the long-running Abba musical *Mamma Mia!*, director Phyllida Lloyd rehearsed the new actors as if it were a new show. The writer Catherine Johnson kept a show diary: 'March 2000: Our new cast takes over – and it's a triumph. I love the way they have re-invented their characters and brought a new freshness to the show.'

Long-running business teams also have to search continually for improvements to satisfy their customers and fend off competitors. This involves continuous learning, frequent revitalizing and ongoing regeneration. Sometimes it will involve you bringing in new members of the 'cast'. This may change the whole nature of your team. You will need to invest time and attention in developing the new team in order that it can perform outstandingly.

DISCOVER WHAT THE CRITICS SAY

Performing teams live or die at the hands of their critics. They are often dependent on them to help generate business. Yet can you imagine launching your own team's activities, having an inspection team in on the first day, and seeing an assessment of your performance printed in the press and talked about in the media? Such is the pressure that theatre teams face.

There is some value in it. You may not agree with the critics and their judgements, but occasionally they make observations that help you see through a blind spot. Similarly, you may benefit from inviting inputs from other departments, clients and suppliers.

What about internal critics? Team meetings are the perfect place for the team to be self-critical. What could we have done better? What can we learn from a recent failure? It's a chance to reflect on what people have discovered from tackling difficulties and how to grow from them.

Don't forget the bouquets either. Sharing successes and triumphs is just as important. Have a space at meetings for individuals to share these, first, so that they can be acknowledged and, second, to enable the team to learn from best practice.

Celebrate achievements

When a performance goes well the members of the audience applaud to show their wholehearted appreciation. If they have thoroughly enjoyed the show, they might even cheer, whistle, stand up, stamp their feet and generally go wild with pleasure and gratitude. Not a bad feeling for the recipient! Yet it is not just performers who value recognition and appreciation – it is a basic human need.

While it may be tricky to replicate standing ovations in most workplaces, it is certainly possible to provide many opportunities for fulsome appreciation. First, however, you need to spot the deserving action. Individuals in teams often complain that their

> 'Having the critics praise you is like having the hangman say you've got a pretty neck.'
> Eli Wallach, actor/director

WHAT ARE YOU PROUD OF TODAY?

There is a real need to ensure that people's contributions are not ignored and to focus on achievements. The team meeting is a perfect place to spend a few moments appreciating what people have done.

You could:

★ Ask everyone to boast about something they've achieved that they're pleased with.

★ Ask people to boast on behalf of others in the team who may have done something special.

★ Have presents for any exceptional effort on behalf of a team member.

★ Have a box of goodies that can be awarded by anyone to any other team member to acknowledge a special action.

★ Recognize and celebrate the end of a period of work or a project.

If your team doesn't do anything to recognize and appreciate performance, people will eventually feel neglected. The whole team can soon dwindle into an everyday, run-of-the-mill outfit that will never be capable of dramatic performance.

---

contributions go unnoticed. Ideally the team leader picks these up and draws them to everyone's attention, but it is a two-way process. Team members also have a responsibility to highlight actions they have taken of which they are proud.

Recognition by your team of what people are achieving becomes highly affirming and reinforces an expectation of outstanding, not merely competent, performance. Such acknowledgement must come from the heart, nevertheless. It is counter-productive if it is forced or artificial.

One way of ensuring enough recognition, as we saw earlier, is to keep dividing the work into chunks to deliver a regular diet of 'endings'. These milestones mark individual and team progress and people look forward to reaching them. They provide perfect opportunities for you to recognize contributions and celebrate successes.

Of course, there are always shy people who really can't stand such public recognition. Nobody should be forced into receiving a level of acknowledgement that is embarrassing or humiliating. There are many ways of showing appreciation, and for those who are averse to celebrity a low-key 'thank-you' may well be enough.

Nevertheless, there is something about an event that has a powerful impact – not merely on the person, but on the team and on the whole company.

> 'If you want something to grow, pour champagne on it.'
> CEO, Alberto-Culver

Produce a sense of occasion

Dramatic team performance deserves special recognition. And theatrical occasions give the team a chance to stop for a moment and savour what has happened, as well as providing something really memorable. Why do such events promote outstanding performance when the occasion itself may be a contrivance? Mainly it allows you time to notice that something special is happening and deserves to be honoured, whether it is a specific work achievement or an anniversary of someone's tenure in the organization. Each can be highlighted to provide an opportunity for the team to meet and celebrate.

> 'Awards are like piles, sooner or later every bum gets one.'
> Maureen Lipman, actor

The spirit of Christmas need not be confined to an annual festival, and the office outing need not be only once a year. You don't always need masses of money and high-profile situations to create a special moment. Maybe it could be getting something published in the house magazine, taking five minutes to mark an achievement, arranging an awayday, having an ice-lolly break in hot weather, conducting an award ceremony or going out for lunch together. Whatever it takes, you can make a commemorative event out of it.

What about you? If you've read this far and perhaps tried out some of the ideas in this book, you have shown a real commitment to improving your own and other people's performance. Why not find a way to celebrate such dedication? Enjoy yourself – our thoughts and thanks are with you!

Create an ACE reputation

So, ACE teams are aligned, creative and exploring. Though they may not last for ever, anyone who has been a member of such a team never forgets the experience. Performance is only one of the benefits for the outstanding team. Another is being part of a community of exceptional colleagues, as well as experiencing a sense of closeness and connection. As actor Lynn Redgrave says, 'What's nice is that you can meet twenty years later and pick up as if you have never left them.'

And such teams build reputations. Certainly actors are proud to announce that they were part of a particular production or theatre company during a certain era. Teams provide special opportunities for success, and if yours isn't performing well at the moment then it's time to take transformative action.

INTERVAL

THE PLOT SO FAR...

Act II was all about getting your team's act together. It outlined what makes an ACE team, one that is aligned, creative and exploring. Each scene explored one of those aspects of team performance.

★   Scene 1: Team alignment means that there is a collective commitment to teamworking. You have the right mix of people offering a diversity of approach, yet sharing the same values. Everyone needs to be going in the same direction, with clear roles and tight organization.

★   Scene 2: Creativity is what the team is for – to produce more than the sum of its parts. This means eliminating the factors that kill creativity, running 'dramatic' meetings where everyone is contributing, and valuing improvisation where people accept and build on each other's ideas. And individual team members bring all of themselves to the enterprise, especially their curiosity and sense of wonder in a playful environment.

★   Scene 3: Exploring is when the team takes its performance out into the world. Its members use an adventurous spirit to take risks and add value to their stakeholders. They learn from successes and failures and grow from the experience. And they celebrate!

Again, the interval allows us time to go out and about and see how people are implementing the ideas covered in Act II in their workplaces.

BEHIND THE SCENES

In which Serge tries a new approach to running a team meeting

SERGE: It's my turn to chair the meeting this month. I want to address some of the concerns you've raised recently. And that means running this meeting slightly differently this time.

PETER: You've been reading those management books again, haven't you?

SERGE: Could be! Anyway, you'll notice there's an agenda item called 'Boasting'.

AMANDA: Boasting! Not sure I like the sound of that.

SERGE: Well, several of us have been complaining that often our contribution goes unnoticed and unrecognized. I think that's partly because we don't even know what some team members are up to.

PETER: Dead right there. I feel really in the dark about what some of you are doing these days.

SERGE: So here's our chance to tell each other what we've been doing – what we're proud about. And if you feel shy talking about your own achievements, then perhaps someone else in the team will highlight them.

Let's also separate items where we need to make a decision from those needing some creative exploration. You'll see I've set aside 15 minutes on the agenda for us to...

AMANDA: *(Interrupting)* We can read the agenda, Serge, it says 'Brainstorming about the new customer service policy'.

SERGE: Thanks Amanda, if you'll let me finish. Lots of you have also said that you're fed up with people talking over each other all the time and, er, interrupting. So I'm introducing what's called a 'talking stick' *(pulling it out of a bag)*. The idea is that you only talk when you're holding it. If you don't have it in your hand you have to stay quiet. We won't use it all the time, but if I notice we're all talking at once, then I'll introduce it.

Right, let's get on with it. Your full attention please. No doodling, no conversations on the side, no sniping and no nodding off! Let's make this meeting really productive.

Rather than being a chance for the team to add value to each other, meetings are often treated mechanistically, as people coming together just to manage operational tasks. Serge has given thought to this meeting and clearly intends to put his stamp on it. That doesn't mean that all meetings should be like this, but he is clearly determined to keep all the team members conscious and contributing.

In which Gill provides some conflict resolution

GILL: Stella and Kareem, I realize that you two are having problems working well together. Well, I can't afford people on my team who don't contribute to each other's performance. I can't just let these things fester and get worse, so I need to know what's going on. Let's hear first from you, Kareem, how does it look from marketing?

KAREEM: I haven't got much of a problem, actually.

STELLA: *(Interrupting)* Oh really?

GILL: Listen, I want each person to speak without being interrupted. You'll both have your say. I'm here to ensure that happens. You were saying, Kareem?

KAREEM: I authorised spending on a new advert. The invoice arrived and Stella stormed over to my desk, waving it in my face.

STELLA: I didn't storm!

KAREEM: Yes you did, it's you people in finance throwing your weight around as usual.

GILL: Cut it out, you two. Let's get back to the important part. So Stella challenged you about the spending. Why was that a problem? Was it the way she did it? Or the fact that she did it at all?

KAREEM: Both. It's my budget. I can spend it how I like, without Stella interfering.

GILL: OK. Stella, let's hear your take on the situation.

STELLA: I'm sick of receiving invoices for marketing spend that I haven't been told about. How on earth can I manage the cash flow of this organization when I'm always getting invoices out of the blue?

KAREEM: *(Interrupting)* They're in my budget!

GILL: You've had your say, Kareem. Now please let's hear Stella's point of view. Uninterrupted.

KAREEM: OK.

STELLA: I've no intention of interfering with your budget, Kareem. But I need to know what you're spending and when.

Freeze – Gill's thoughts go something like this:

GILL: Ah! I'm starting to see what the problem is. Kareem feels threatened that his power to control his budget is being questioned, and therefore his freedom to make decisions. And Stella is frightened that her ability to manage cash flow is jeopardized by lack of information from Kareem. OK, so there might be some personality stuff involved here as well, but if I can get them to see it from the other's point of view, and we can sort out the procedural problems, we stand a good chance of healing this relationship.

- -

Guideline 1: Relationship problems need to be addressed, not avoided.

Guideline 2: Problems not dealt with will probably only get worse.

Guideline 3: Be wary of blaming problems on a so-called personality clash; often the problem lies elsewhere.

Guideline 4: Look for a structural problem that may be causing the conflict.

Guideline 5: By highlighting the structural issue you make it easier for both parties to see the other person's point of view.

- -

In which Frances faces a team challenge

FRANCES: I've called an extraordinary team meeting because we're in an extraordinary situation. Next week the inspectors call! I know a number of you are dreading the prospect.

NEIL: You can say that again. *(General murmurs of apprehension)*

FRANCES: As you know, they'll be with us for the week and on the whole, I trust that if we just go about our business in our normal way, we'll be successful.

I want to let you know how I see it. I really feel this is a fantastic challenge. It's a chance for us to pull together and demonstrate the quality of the work we do. We'd be crazy if we didn't seize this opportunity. But that means not only doing what we normally do but making an extra effort.

JIM: What are you talking about? What more can we possibly be doing? We've been working our socks off all week. *(General rumbles of agreement)*

FRANCES: I know you have. But it would be crazy not to go that extra bit further and get the report we deserve. And I won't be asking you to do anything I'm not prepared to do myself.

PAM: That's always true of you, Fran.

FRANCES: Thanks. Next weekend I'll be here, both Saturday and Sunday. I want us to clean things up a bit. I'd like us to look for imaginative ways to demonstrate the creativity that goes on in the school. It's not about putting on a show for the inspectors, but it is about showing ourselves at our best. So, any volunteers to join me at the weekend?

PUNAM: I can't come in on the Saturday I'm afraid, Fran, but I could make Sunday. I'd like to rearrange the reading room and finish off the catalogue system. It's something I've been meaning to do for ages. Now would be a good time.

NEIL: I'm the other way round. I can't do the Sunday, but you'll certainly see me here on Saturday. I want to go through the stockroom. It's fine as long as nobody opens the door, but as soon as they do they'll see a real shambles. You can rely on me to get that done.

FRANCES: That's just what I'm looking for. It's the difference between ordinary and outstanding. Let's really impress them. What else could we be doing? Come on, people, get thinking...

A challenge is a great way to pull a team together to produce exceptional performance. It's an opportunity for the team to add value to each other and produce more than the sum of their parts. Nevertheless, it demands a commitment from everyone involved, and the team leader certainly needs to lead the way.

Frances is willing to work as hard as any of the team, if not harder. And yet she also makes it clear that she can't do it on her own. She is inviting the others to support her and it's obvious how they can contribute.

If you want that exceptional effort from your team:

★ Describe the situation.
★ Explain why a Herculean effort is needed.
★ Spell out the exact results expected.
★ Clarify how long the exceptional effort is required.
★ Talk about the implications of succeeding.
★ Communicate the price of failure.
★ Ask for help.
★ Lead the way.

What about the bigger picture? I want to make an impact on the whole organization. How do I produce dramatic performance across my company?

Executive

Anticipating the start of Act III, our producer and company executive contemplate issues prompted by what they've been watching.

EXECUTIVE: It doesn't seem to matter how well I personally perform, or even how well my team does, we just keep getting blocked higher up the line. I wish I knew how to make a real difference there.

PRODUCER: That must be frustrating! Unless you feel everything is pulling in the same direction it can all seem a waste of effort.

EXECUTIVE: Don't I know it! But changing it all is a huge mountain to climb.

PRODUCER: It's rather like putting on a stage show, only bigger.

EXECUTIVE: What do you mean?

PRODUCER: OK, what sort of production are you aiming for? Obviously you want something outstanding, but you have to be much more specific than that.

EXECUTIVE: So we need to define what outstanding really means?

PRODUCER: Exactly. Here's where using theatre can really help.

EXECUTIVE: How?

PRODUCER: By taking a step back and looking at your organization from an entirely different perspective. For example, imagine sitting in the front row of the stalls here in this theatre and watching the everyday proceedings of your company.

EXECUTIVE: The lights, the stage, the chaos…

PRODUCER: Come on! I know it's not quite like that. But if you were seeing it as a stage performance, what sort of drama would you be watching?

EXECUTIVE: A bit like the film *Gladiator*, I reckon. My talented team against the full might of a corrupt Roman Empire!

PRODUCER: How do you feel about that, especially your role in it? Are you central to what's happening, or are you just a bit-part player in someone else's production?

EXECUTIVE: That's a useful perspective. So you reckon I'm like a Hollywood star who can change the entire company?

PRODUCER: I'm not sure about the Hollywood star bit, but once you've decided to make a difference there's a lot you can do. Let's watch and see.

The lights dim and the curtain rises on Act III. This act reveals the three key leadership capabilities required to transform your workplace. They are:

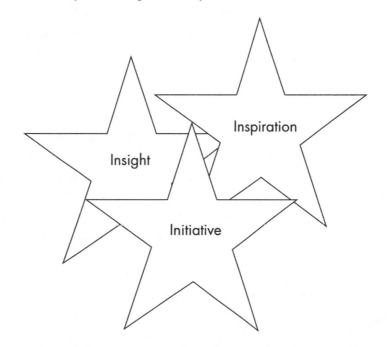

Act III therefore consists of three scenes, each exploring what is required to produce dramatic performance in an organization:

- ★ Scene 1 – *Organizational insight*: how to understand your talent and see what is needed.
- ★ Scene 2 – *Organizational inspiration*: how to inspire and involve people.
- ★ Scene 3 – *Organizational initiative*: how to implement with a ruthless commitment to delivery.

SCENE 1
ORGANIZATIONAL INSIGHT

Everyone can use insight to improve performance. Not only do we all possess insight, we can also nurture and improve it. To develop your insight:

★ *Know yourself*: explore who you are, what impact you have on people, how you need to change.
★ *Understand others*: discover what people need, why they do what they do, what would help them perform better.
★ *See the situation*: uncover what is really happening – in the office, in the company, in the marketplace, in the industry, with the competition, in the future. What needs to happen next?

'Some actors hold up a picture and say "look at me". I want to hold up a mirror to the audience and say "look at you".'
Michael Caine, actor

Part of improving insight requires us to reflect on how others see us. If we can see the truth about ourselves, we also stand a chance of seeing the truth about others and the situation around us. This insight allows us to understand how to generate improved performance.

Reflection has long been the route to creating better understanding and hence having the ability to change the world around us. Russian playwright Anton Chekhov, for example, wanted his plays to reflect people's lives back to the audience so that they might better understand themselves. He argued, 'Man will become better when you show him what he is like.'

More recently, the artistic director of the UK's National Theatre, Nicholas Hytner, argued: 'As a nation, we think we know who we are, but we need to find out what we're becoming. It's a tremendous opportunity for a national theatre, an exhilarating challenge to hold the mirror up to the nation. In the reflection, we'll find new generations, new communities, a society bursting with fresh sources of life and energy. I want all that energy on our stages. I want the National Theatre to find out what "national" means.'

Know yourself

Leadership is autobiographical. Who you are is how you lead. The better you know yourself, the more confidence you will possess for being a leader. Astute leaders constantly want to know what is happening within themselves and how it affects their outward behaviour.

Becoming self-aware is not merely important for actors. It is firmly embedded in current management and leadership thinking. Nor is it particularly mystical or entirely self-absorbing. It is about understanding your personality, its strengths and weaknesses and its impact on others. But such awareness does require an actor's intensity of focus.

Says psychologist Brian Bates: 'The actor's journey is identical to the path we all tread through life. But an actor travels much further along it. By exploring other characters, actors explore themselves and by sharing the experience of actors, we can understand our own experiences.'

The self-awareness that performers rely on to produce outstanding performance is a process of introspection that leaves nothing unexplored. By delving deeply, an actor acquires more resources for playing roles authentically. The journey to increased self-awareness need not be a lonely one. Actors receive continual feedback from their director and fellow actors in rehearsal, as well as the instant reactions of their audience and critiques from reviewers. Business replicates this by fostering 360 degree feedback tools, assessment centres, staff surveys and other ways for leaders to test how they see themselves against the reality of how others experience them.

'Being an actor, you sometimes have to ask yourself questions you don't even want to know the answer to.'
Kevin Spacey, actor

QUESTIONS TO YOURSELF

To increase your self-awareness, keep asking:

★   Why did I do that?
★   What effect did I have?
★   Why did that work?
★   How could I do that better?
★   What went wrong with what I did?
★   That worked, how could I do it again?
★   How did people react to what I said or did?
★   How am I feeling right now?

Understand others

MANAGER: Welcome to your first day at work here. This is your computer and there's the manual for it. If you really want to get the best out of it, study that manual.

EMPLOYEE: Thanks.

MANAGER: And this is a scanner that you can use with it. It'll do far more than you can imagine, so read the manual.

EMPLOYEE: OK.

MANAGER: We have this terrific phone system here. This phone on your desk is full of new-fangled tricks you'll find useful. By the way, its manual is in your drawer here. Read it and you'll know how to get it to perform properly.

EMPLOYEE: Thanks.

MANAGER: Now, where's *your* manual?

EMPLOYEE: I'm not sure I quite understand what you mean.

MANAGER: All these manuals tell us how to get the best performance out of the equipment. The manuals come in the box when they arrive. You've just arrived. I assume you've got a manual tucked away somewhere? Otherwise, how am I going to get you to perform properly?

Of course, human beings don't arrive with instructions on how they work best. Instead, you have to create a 'manual' for each of your people. Even as you gather the information, you know that it will require an immediate update because human beings keep changing.

Director Richard Eyre comments: 'A director is usually a cook: he assembles the best ingredients, follows his recipe and serves it up as impressively as he can. Occasionally, and very rarely, a director is an alchemist, transforming dross into theatrical, even real gold. More often, however, a director is like a dowser or water diviner, trying to detect the potential that lies below the surface of an actor's talent.'

As we gather our working manuals on other people, we almost certainly see them inaccurately. Our history and our experience affect our perception. We tend to perceive people through a fog of beliefs, prejudices, interpretations, judgements, interests and blind spots. Our own needs govern how much reality we absorb. So it can be hard to see people as they truly are, untainted by our assumptions about them, let alone to see them in fresh and different ways.

Do you want to release people's potential? Then there is no substitute for meeting people, getting to know more about them, and being constantly curious about what will help them perform better. It's a continuous process of observation, exploration and testing.

See the situation

Unfortunately, we tend to leap to assumptions and judgements without first making the effort to obtain a full picture of what is happening around us. We tend to take the easy route and rely on habitual views, or we complicate them with our interpretations and miss the obvious.

> 'There is a crying, almost screaming, need of a great worldwide human effort to know ourselves and each other a great deal better.'
> Tennessee Williams, playwright

> 'If you can keep your head when all about you are losing theirs, it's just possible you haven't grasped the situation.'
> Jean Kerr, writer

SHERLOCK HOLMES: Watson, as we lie here, look up at the sky and tell me what you see.

DR WATSON: I see millions of stars, Holmes.

SHERLOCK HOLMES: And what does that tell you?

DR WATSON: Astronomically, it tells me that there are millions of galaxies. Astrologically, I observe that Saturn is in Leo. Horologically, I deduce that the time is 3.15 am. Theologically, I can see that God is all powerful. Meteorologically, I suspect tomorrow will be a beautiful day. What does it tell you, Holmes?

SHERLOCK HOLMES: Watson, my dear fellow, it tells me someone has stolen our tent!

It is easy to miss reality because we are wrapped up in our own view of the world. This is why teams can be so useful and productive, since each person contributes a unique perspective unseen by others. When you remain open to other people's perspectives, you reduce and may even eliminate any blind spots you possess.

Highly effective leaders acquire their acute grasp of reality through being open to others. They seem to know exactly what is happening around them not through the magic of charisma, but by absorbing and interpreting information. It is this that allows them to direct what needs to be done. In practice, they are ready to adopt or discard views, prejudices, assumptions, beliefs and interpretations in order to try to see reality.

How do you begin to see with clarity? Start with the facts. Without information you cannot expect to make sense of what is happening. Factual information builds a more accurate picture of the current situation. Only then can you go beyond that, to see other important pieces of the jigsaw. There is seldom enough information and it is important to be aware of the danger of paralysis by analysis.

What do the facts tell you about what's going on? Next, what do they imply for the future; that is, what can you infer from them?

'We don't see things as they are; we see them as we are.'
Anaïs Nin, writer

OBSERVE, PERCEIVE AND WONDER

It takes practice to develop an ability to see clearly and therefore choose appropriate initiatives that surprise and delight. A useful way of practising is the acting exercise of observe, perceive and wonder. This stimulates a rounded view of a situation.

★   First, start with facts (*observe*).
★   Second, explore feelings and interpretations about a situation (*perceive*).
★   Third, use instinct to decide what might be hidden from view (*wonder*).

This approach allows you to separate out what is factually true from what is embellished by your own subjective influence. You may well be right in your interpretations and beliefs, but good leadership starts with knowing which is which.

Apply your natural curiosity, use your desire for improvement and put your natural creative powers to work. Later you may reflect on what you did and call it foresight.

Develop foresight

Inspirational leaders see what is needed for the future. They seem to show uncanny prescience. Yet this knack does not depend on having a crystal ball but on interpreting the present, and staying fully alert to external factors and their possible impact. It also stems from listening to people and using networks to stay in touch. Through remaining absolutely in the present and tuning in to other people, you can see opportunities that others may miss. As someone once said, 'Foresight is just hindsight ahead of time.'

Who would have thought that a musical about Eva Peron (*Evita*) would be so successful? Or one based on a Victor Hugo novel (*Les Miserables*)? Or a play with two actors adapted from a

'A hunch is creativity trying to tell you something.'
Frank Capra, director

THE FORESIGHT SAGA

To develop more accurate foresight, engage your colleagues in unravelling puzzles such as:

★ How do we stay ahead of the game?
★ What new developments are over the horizon?
★ What contingencies can we plan for?
★ What if current trends were suddenly reversed?

mystery story (*Woman in Black*)? Or a musical based on the songs of a 1980s pop group (*Mamma Mia!*)? The people that did think so made a great deal of money.

Like charisma, foresight lies buried under a mound of mystique. How does it work, which leaders have it and which don't, and can anyone develop it? Because it seems so mysterious we attribute all kinds of explanations to its occurrence. As Arthur C. Clarke noted: 'Any sufficiently advanced technology is indistinguishable from magic.' What may be labelled prescience usually turns out to be merely acute perception.

Brazilian director Augustus Boal expresses it as follows: 'Theatre is the capacity possessed by human beings – not by animals – to observe themselves in action. Humans are capable of seeing themselves in the act of seeing, of thinking their emotions, of being moved by their thoughts. They can see themselves here and imagine themselves there; they can see themselves today and imagine themselves tomorrow.'

Business people usually see themselves as hardened realists. So dreaming, fantasy and imagining tend to be consigned to others, such as specialist departments, researchers or outside experts. Yet fantasizing can be highly productive and an essential part of what others regard as exhibiting foresight.

Developing foresight that creates business opportunities requires a mix of hard work and playfulness. It's an odd combination. By encouraging your people to ask creative and challenging questions, you are more likely to reveal new opportunities. This is the value of the 'What if?' questions discussed earlier. What if we could do it ten times better? What if we could do it in half the time? What if we were twice as efficient? What if we were the leader in our industry? What if we had to relocate? What if one of our competitors suddenly developed a completely new product?

Creative thought experiments often produce usable ideas about the future. 'What if we mainly sold our airline tickets on the internet?' asked easyJet's Stelios Haji-Ioannou. With incentives to buy online, over 80 per cent of the airline's sales shifted to the web within two years. In retrospect, when people say that a leader has great foresight, what they really mean is that they have an ability to dream with their feet on the ground. The question 'What if we could make a quality Swiss watch ten times cheaper than normal?' produced the immensely successful Swatch brand.

So foresight means staying fully alert to what is happening around you. It is not merely about insisting on the metrics; equally important is where you focus your attention. Actors have many useful exercises to develop their sensory acuity: a heightened awareness of the information that your senses are giving you all the time. Often we are so busy that we don't register this information and fail to make conscious choices about where we put our attention.

Sensing and anticipating allow you to respond to an intuitive sense of danger. Although companies can fail through no fault of their own, many hit the wall because senior management had simply gone to sleep or didn't have the experience to recognize a crisis until it was too late. For example, when accountancy firm Arthur Andersen faced a crisis of confidence in which its entire organizational integrity was in doubt, its leadership seemed to fail to respond, essentially going into denial. Similarly, market trends

> 'The tragedy of life is that we understand it backwards, but we have to live it forwards.'
> Søren Kierkegaard, philosopher

NIGHTMARE SCENARIOS

One extremely fruitful 'What if?' approach requires a team to select an important issue that needs to be resolved and make a video about it. The team researches, writes, acts and produces several short dramatizations. The first depicts 'The present situation'; the second shows 'The nightmare scenario', bringing to life what might occur if nothing is done about the problem. Finally, in 'The revelation', the team acts out a new reality as if the problem had been removed.

Using creativity, performance and imagining the future in this way can be enormous fun, stimulating everyone to see the situation more realistically. This is a guided visualization, creative group brainstorm and behavioural change exercise all rolled into one. By acting out the imagined future, people see and live through the possible dangers. It enables them to alter long-standing behaviour, to arrive at practical ways of resolving their differences, and to move towards implementing 'The revelation' that they had only imagined at first.

alone cannot explain the hole that retailer Marks & Spencer dug itself into before being rescued by a new leadership that more fully understood what was happening within and around the company. Success had bred complacency.

Scenario planning is the business version of playing the 'What if?' game. It can sometimes help prevent disasters by helping people imagine the worst and how to respond to it. This gives you an advantage over those who simply sit back and wait for it to happen. Just how bad could things get? What is your worst nightmare and how would you perform should the worst come to pass? By involving your team in thinking about such questions, you can galvanize its members into producing creative solutions.

SCENE 2
ORGANIZATIONAL INSPIRATION

'You learn a lot from acting,' says Logica chief executive Martin Read. He values the contribution the theatre can make to his job, explaining: 'The show must go on. You'll muddle through somehow, getting on with people... what else is management, for God's sake? So I think it's an excellent training ground.'

Read tends to quote from Shakespeare's *Henry V*, before the battle of Agincourt: 'We few, we happy few, we band of brothers.' He declares it 'the best motivational speech ever. Every manager should read it. It makes you think how do you motivate people? I spend my whole life acting. Any good chief executive has to be good at acting. That's what we do.'

Unlike a director in the business world whose title denotes legal responsibilities, a theatre director does exactly as the name suggests: provides direction. This involves setting an overall vision for the production and ensuring the alignment of all participants, including lighting and costume designers, stage management, and of course the actors. Skilled theatre directors do all of this while encouraging people to perform at their best. People become highly frustrated if there is no regular direction and there is a collective sigh of relief when it finally emerges.

Just as actors need to know how the play turns out and how it will be mounted, so your people need to know where you are leading them and how you intend to get them there. This allows them to make their own decisions on whether to sign up for the journey. Each individual comes to terms with this direction at a personal level, engaging their heart as well as their rational mind. People commit their inner spirit to a company only when there is a compelling chemistry pulling them in a rewarding direction.

> 'A group wants to be led. If it is not led, somebody replaces the leader. Actors didn't go to work with groups, they went to work with the people who led those groups – Joan Littlewood, Ariane Mnouchkine, Peter Brook. They wanted leaders.'
> Peter Hall, director

If you're a leader, then lead!

André Previn once exploded the myth of the all-powerful and controlling maestro conductor. In a memorable televised demonstration, he left the podium halfway through conducting a piece of music. Without his commanding figure, the audience expected the orchestra to fall apart. Instead, the musicians played on beautifully, completing the piece with aplomb.

Previn showed that that he was not there to dictate every moment of playing. Instead, his role was more like that of a theatre director. The prime role of both director and conductor is to provide direction – that is, where the ensemble is going – and inspire great performance. That is leadership. Neither exists to 'manage' the situation.

Despite the obvious differences between the work of theatre and the theatre of work, leadership in both cases is about drawing out a great performance through attracting, spotting, recruiting, releasing and developing talent. But no leader works in isolation.

An actor playing a king, for instance, soon realizes that you cannot do this on your own and still exude authority. You need the rest of the cast to treat you with suitable respect. Wearing a crown and robes and strutting regally around the stage only work if the others do suitable grovelling and submissive acting. Only then do you appear majestic.

Leadership is a relationship between the leader and their supporters. We prefer the notion of supporters rather than followers. Followers imply passive minions, unquestioning and dutiful. Supporters make choices, buying into a vision or committing to a particular set of values and aims. They need to be proactive, creative, questioning, decisive and resilient. So when they choose to offer their support they, too, are exercising a form of leadership.

> 'He played the king all evening under the constant fear that someone else was about to play the ace.'
> Eugene Field, critic, of an actor playing King Lear

Everyone in an organization can and should play some kind of leadership role. It may not be strategic, nor will everyone have the desire to be a formal leader. Yet each member of your cast needs to add value by demonstrating leadership through their actions.

Leadership + supporters + the situation = results

Leadership is about inspiration, not motivation. The reality is that you don't need to motivate someone to do what they already want to do. So it is clearly your job as a leader to provide an environment where that self-motivation is focused on the job in hand.

Finding time and space to talk about inspiration is meat and drink to people in the theatre because for them it is a way of life. In business, though, the whole concept may be counter to the culture. A recent UK survey asked 1,500 executives what they most wanted from their leaders. Around half said that above all they desired inspiration, yet fewer than one in ten said that they got it.

The challenge for business is first to make it possible to talk about inspiration as an essential component of high-level performance, and second to find ways to turn it into an operational tool that creates exceptional results. But getting something as intangible as inspiration onto the corporate agenda can be an uphill struggle.

Inspiration alters people inwardly so that they think and act differently, often performing beyond their own and other people's expectations. They *feel* the difference. And while it may be difficult, what would you rather be doing: striving for the mundane, or going for something special?

There is a myth that inspiration strikes unexpectedly. Yet most inventive ideas or 'eureka' moments normally stem from careful preparation. Put inspiration to work in your organization by researching your own personal sources of inspiration. To inspire others, you must first inspire yourself.

SOURCES OF INSPIRATION

Take some time right now to explore what inspires you. Start listing books, events, films, poems, people, quotes, places, paintings, experiences and whatever you find uplifting and exceptionally exciting. As you recall these, or even read or see them again, you become aware of why they inspire you and the feelings they generate.

Now consider what could produce similar feelings about the performance in your own company. What would need to be happening for you to feel inspired?

You could try a similar process with your colleagues. You might share some examples of inspiration and discuss how they make you feel. Disclosing personal information in this way helps build better working relationships. Suddenly people seem human and capable of being affected emotionally, and indeed inspired.

Starting a conversation about inspiration puts your collective attention on the subject. Then, by extending it to focus on workplace performance, you start a new dialogue that could identify routes to truly exceptional results. You can create a stream of productive ideas for transforming how you serve customers, present products and deal with staff.

> 'Inspiration is a guest who doesn't like to visit lazy people.'
> Pyotr Il'yich Tchaikovsky, composer

Once you have found your own source of inspiration, you can begin inspiring others to produce dramatic success. There is much to be done to make this happen. While it is not all about shouting from the hilltops, it will certainly involve you in communicating your vision and exciting people with your grand scheme.

En route to inspiring their production teams, stage directors will do practically anything to convey what they want. Director Jonathan Miller, for instance, keeps extensive files and uses his large personal collection of art books to spark his designers' imagination or inspire actors regarding period and mood. Working on a Chekhov play, one director conducted the read-through on the first day of rehearsal over a Russian-style lunch complete with samovar and vodka. In rehearsals, directors often use images,

CREATE LEGENDS

What are the good stories in your organization? Every enterprise has its stories, but the ones people remember are often those of disaster or humiliation. Instead, you can highlight uplifting examples of best practice or outstanding service and spread them around. They soon become the company's legends.

People share these experiences on workshops and company awaydays. Fellow workers are normally delighted to hear what others have been up to. As a leader, you can encourage this focus on potentially legendary incidents, whether it is in a team meeting or in the pub. Either way, it becomes part of an inspiring culture. Marriott Hotels even ran a successful advertising campaign based on stories of how it treated its customers.

metaphors, stories, 3D models of the future stage, coloured costume designs and other devices to convey their vision of the play and get people excited.

Walt Disney reduced his animators to tears by personally acting out the entire story of *Snow White* for several hours. When he ground to an exhausted halt, everyone had mentally seen the entire production and they were inspired. They talked about it for decades afterwards. The true power of what you want to achieve lies in communicating it effectively to others.

In their polemical book *Funky Business*, Ridderstråle and Nordström say that CEOs should be 'CSOs – Chief Storytelling Officers'. Stories of best practice circulating through the organization prove important because they tell us what others are doing well and because legends excite and success stories inspire. They also help people see where the company script is heading.

IKEA's founder Ingvar Kamprad regularly uses storytelling. Many people across the burgeoning global company know the legend of Kamprad travelling by airport buses to save money on taxis and limousines. This simple story, told in a single sentence, has

> 'I'm an assistant storyteller. It's like being a waiter or a gas station attendant, but I'm waiting on six million people a week, if I'm lucky.'
> Harrison Ford, actor

TALKING PICTURES

To win people's hearts and minds when presenting your vision, communicate directly and personally. Theatre experience says:

★ Speak from the heart.
★ Use specific examples.
★ Adopt metaphors, stories and images.
★ Demonstrate your personal commitment.
★ To invoke feelings use descriptive and evocative language.
★ Explain how your audience can contribute and what's in it for them.

powerful ramifications and a clear message. Here is a rich man still in touch with reality, who is concerned with value, who is the same as the rest of us. Kamprad's bus journeys encapsulate the values embodied by IKEA. Strangely, few people seem to care whether the stories are true or not. Metaphors have power – myths outweigh facts.

> 'What would he do, had he the motive and the cue for passion that I have?'
> *Hamlet,*
> William Shakespeare

Be passionate

Listen to Julian Richer talking about selling at his hi-fi chain Richer Sounds; or James Dyson enthusing about his unique cleaner; or The Body Shop's Anita Roddick explaining about other cultures in the developing world; or Nick Park of Aardman Animations on the potential of plasticine in animation; or Warren Buffett on sound investment; or Michael Eisner on creativity at Disney. These people are hungry to be outstanding in one particular area. They also want to inspire an organization that is permeated by passion.

US consultant and author Richard Chang believes that 'passion is the single most powerful competitive advantage an organization can claim in building its success'. He claims the following tangible benefits of passion in business:

★ Provides direction and focus.
★ Creates energy.
★ Fosters creativity.
★ Heightens performance.
★ Inspires action.
★ Attracts employees and customers.
★ Builds loyalty.
★ Unites the organization.
★ Provides a critical edge.
★ Brings the organization to a higher plane.

Perhaps passion is too scary for your company? Organizations that want their people to feel passionate about what they do seem rather rare. It is almost as if passion poses a threat to order and control – which in fact it may.

People who are passionate about something tend to challenge what is happening around them or be less than totally obedient. Like a virus, passion is infectious. Yet if you really want above-average performance, people need to feel passionate about what they do for your business.

Generate excitement

The surest way to persuade the best people to stick around is to make work exciting. Inspired leaders create a stimulating atmosphere around them. As with a play, make sure your staff want to know what will happen next in the unfolding plot. While not deliberately unsettling people, make the unexpected the norm. Talented people want to stay if they feel that something new is always possible. And this applies to every area of the company's activities.

CONTAINED PASSION

Passion in business does not have to be loud or gung-ho. When you ask people to recall experiences of high emotion in their life, they will usually reconnect with feelings of joy or sadness. These may be deeply felt, but quietly. Once the person experiences them, however, the feelings become instantly visible to others.

When people connect with their passion – whether childhood experiences, moments of success, watching a baby being born, climbing a mountain, suffering a bereavement – their facial colour changes, their eyes are affected, their breathing alters and their whole physical being subtly transforms.

To play a person in love or someone who is grieving, actors must connect with those feelings inside themselves if they are to move the audience in some way. The same is true of leaders who want to communicate excitement about a project or fear of the challenges ahead.

'I have never been drawn to the whodunnit pure and simple: that's an intellectual exercise containing no emotion, you see. Now, suspense acts as a spur and adventure involves audiences' emotions.'
Alfred Hitchcock, director

If you can generate a daily theatre full of excitement, people will want to stick around to see what will happen next. In the pioneering days of the research powerhouse Xerox PARC in California's Santa Clara Valley, few of those who joined did so with the thought of becoming rich, although the company paid them slightly over the odds for their specialist skills. What attracted them was the thrill of being at the cutting edge and pioneering. Years later one of them described the experience as akin to the sheer joy of making the first footprints in a field of virgin snow.

People convey excitement when they really care about something, and theatre techniques can support them. Businesses around the world are bringing in theatre companies to help leaders get in touch with their inspiration and improve their ability to generate excitement. They find that theatre-based development methods are ideal for helping people learn how to produce a natural and

DRAMATIC ORIENTATION

Probably the last thing you expect from a talk by lawyers is an invitation to a line dance. But newcomers to AIR MILES never forgot the crucial legal information that the lawyers successfully conveyed during a memorable line-dancing session.

Excitement pervaded AIR MILES in its heyday. But little of the company's exciting culture came across to newcomers during their week-long induction course. A team set out to change the whole experience, which the project leader aptly described as 'Death by PowerPoint'. Managers from different departments would drop into the induction sessions to deliver a series of boring slides stuffed with endless bullet points. This ordeal lasted for five straight mornings. Just to liven things up, the afternoons were filled with talk about systems.

AIR MILES wanted its induction to embody the culture of the organization. How could the excitement that made people come to work every day enliven and inform the induction experience? The project team concluded that it had to become a more memorable, transforming event that inspired people's understanding of the company they had chosen to join.

The team members decided to theatricalize the experience, making it entirely participative. They adopted a theatrical theme for each step along the journey of an AIR MILE and each department created an interactive session or 'act' for the new joiners that inspired the legal department to teach its message using a line dance. The impact of the new programme was substantial, was felt to reflect the company culture more accurately, and ran regularly every few months.

believable sense of excitement. After all, it's why we go to the theatre – to be moved, stimulated, challenged and inspired.

Drama-based development has increasingly shown that it can unlock people's creative flair to generate excitement and apply it to work. It is more than another faddish attempt to encourage a bit of buzz. Traditionally, groups were whisked off to the mountains or onto yachts to do adventure-based learning. Outdoor

ACTING IT OUT

Specially commissioned plays help companies kick-start the excitement that ultimately generates an inspirational atmosphere. For instance, using semi-professional help a group of employees from GlaxoSmithKline performed a lively Christmas pantomime about a new drug launch to the rest of their division. It triggered as much excitement among the performers as among the members of the audience, who were later able to discuss the issues in the show. They also had fun doing it.

Other cultural issues in a company can be dramatized. For example, sensitive issues such as gender conflicts at work, prejudice and racism, diversity, taking responsibility and customer service have all been dramatized in some form.

And many companies have used the experience of putting on a show for team development, whether it be mounting an opera, performing Shakespeare or playing theatre games.

activities can certainly produce excitement, but provoke a 're-entry' problem when people return to work. The best drama-based development is 'inward-bound' learning rather than 'outward-bound', is just as exciting, and can be transferred more easily to the workplace.

Communicating a vision in a passionate way that generates excitement is a key ingredient in the recipe for inspiring people. But there are many other factors required to persuade people to give of their best, such as sharing values, involvement, coaching and providing recognition.

Add value using values

Values glue an organization together, especially during a period of constant and rapid change, as we saw when discussing teams in Act II. When you can convey your values clearly, it not only enables bet-

WALK THE TALK

Why not talk about the important things in life, rather than conversations being dominated by operational detail? Of course operational issues need to be discussed and decisions made, but not at the expense of what really matters.

Many companies run values workshops, where staff can get together and discuss what they value about the way they work together. Highlighting the key values and what they look like in action, with examples of people embodying them, is a valuable process to move the organization forward.

Solicitors Thomas Eggar ran a series of values workshops with teams and, having discussed and agreed their values, they painted pictures that expressed them as action in the company. Participants agreed that they found the events really valuable and a good reminder of what was important to them. They followed these up with a conference for the whole company, including an exhibition of the pictures.

ter decision making, but can really provide people with excitement and satisfaction.

Some leaders succeed in putting values at the heart of the company and use this to reinforce the overall vision. Natural cosmetics retailer The Body Shop, gourmet sandwich shop Pret A Manger and furniture company IKEA are not merely clear brands, they express the leader's set of values, strongly manifested in the business, and help inspire outstanding performance.

Values statements are not enough on their own. Energy conglomerate Enron boasted of having 'communication, respect, excellence and integrity' as its core values – before it became the largest bankruptcy in US corporate history. And it's not just corruption that distorts values. A recent study showed managers interpreting 'integrity' in 185 ways. So as well as acting out your values, you will need to get absolute clarity of meaning among your people.

CLEAR VALUES

There are plenty of ways to help clarify your values:

★ Explore the values that define high performance within your team.

★ Develop a values statement for your team, including the behaviour you want to see to support the values.

★ Can you understand diversity and individual differences within your team? And can you look at these differences in a non-judgemental way?

★ See if you can harmonize the differences into some core or all-embracing values that you can all share.

★ What action or behaviour expresses the values? How would an outsider recognize them?

The way you behave in supporting the values you espouse is critical, since this determines whether they will radiate outwards. At food group Geest, for example, even though a manager was hitting targets he was asked to leave the company. His boss explained the controversial decision: 'He wasn't supporting our values.' Similarly, at jean manufacturer Levi Strauss, corporate values are embedded in appraisals and managers who meet business targets but score low on values forgo their bonuses.

Involve people

'You don't dare pop out to the toilet,' complained actors working with Joan Littlewood at Theatre Workshop on *Oh! What a Lovely War*, because you might find your part cut during even a short absence. She produced an absorbing rehearsal process where everybody was completely involved. So dynamic were her improvisation and creativity that everything was always changing, depending on different people's contributions. So if you weren't around to contribute, you might do less in the actual performance.

There's plenty you can do to help people feel part of something special. You are only really limited by your imagination. For example, before outsourcing production abroad, James Dyson insisted that everyone starting work made a vacuum cleaner on their first day. This was true from the lowliest member of staff to a non-executive director. 'When you take your self-made vacuum cleaner home,' explained Dyson, 'you get a grasp of the company's *raison d'être*.'

If you want people to produce extraordinary rather than ordinary performance, they have to feel they can make a difference in some way. Many under-performers feel irrelevant to the success of the organization. Everyone in a theatre production knows that their contribution is visible and essential. This has important lessons for business, where many organizations generate mediocre performance simply because individuals feel reduced to a cog, with little direct influence on what's going on around them.

Use theatre-based coaching

For coaching to inspire outstanding performance, you may first have to challenge some conventional views of how it works best, including the often-drawn analogy with sports. Frequently the coach acts as an all-knowing teacher, imparting knowledge and skill to the person on the receiving end. At the other extreme, the coach is an enabler, hardly existing or intervening, just asking open questions of the person being coached. Neither of these seems as useful as theatre-based coaching.

The relationship between the theatre director – the coach – and the actor is one of creative collaboration. Both are involved, but neither knows exactly what will be produced. They embark on a dynamic, creative journey together. For example, according to one person who worked with the renowned Austrian stage director

Max Reinhardt: 'He preferred to draw actors aside and whisper to them privately, saying just the right few words, or offering the precise gesture, to inspire their imaginations.'

One of the main reasons why Russian theatre director Constantin Stanislavsky, the founding father of modern acting, was so influential was that he noticed how real life worked. He used this to steer his dramatic process. For example, he observed how people went about their lives to achieve their *objectives*. He noticed that what made life and drama interesting were the *obstacles* people met and the *actions* they took to overcome them. This approach provides actors with a powerful way of working when rehearsing a play. They explore what happens to their characters and the journey they take throughout a drama. It also provides business people with a useful model for quick and easy coaching at work.

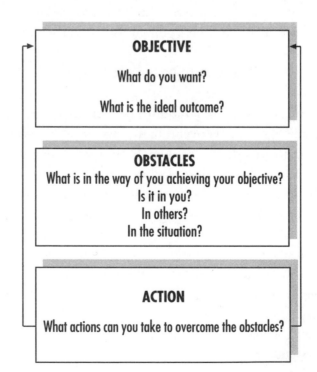

OBJECTIVE

What do you want?

What is the ideal outcome?

OBSTACLES
What is in the way of you achieving your objective?
Is it in you?
In others?
In the situation?

ACTION

What actions can you take to overcome the obstacles?

You can see how it works with a play like Shakespeare's *Hamlet*. Hamlet's *objective* is to avenge his father's death. If he simply went up and killed Claudius, the play would be over in the first ten minutes. Instead, he meets some *obstacles*. There are obstacles in:

★ Himself, his inner turmoil: 'To be, or not to be; that is the question.'
★ Others: 'Frailty, they name is woman!'
★ The situation: 'Something is rotten in the state of Denmark.'

The drama unfolds as we watch him struggling to decide which *actions* he can take to overcome these obstacles. One of those, for instance, is the creative trick of using a play to expose the king's guilt: 'The play's the thing wherein I'll catch the conscience of the king.'

Try using this simple framework of objective, obstacle and action within your business. It is a quick and useful reminder for any manager wanting to coach and support someone. Like Hamlet, you need to be creative in your action-focused solutions.

Coaching really can inspire people and yet it need not take up much of your time. As a leadership style, it provides a transition from command and control to a more supportive and enabling approach. It focuses on developing people, on helping them find their own way to achieve outstanding results. It helps you retain talent, by giving your best people the attention they deserve, assisting them in finding their own way through problem solving, and it also lets you immediately tackle issues as they arise.

You might benefit from some coaching for yourself. The CEO of Chrysalis Entertainment, for example, brought in an executive coach because he was working 18-hour days and had 30 projects on the go. He and his staff worked with the coach every month for two years, defining goals and building strategy from the bottom up. The company went from £1 million to £90 million turnover in six years.

DRAMATIC COACHING

Stage directors have always used different styles of coaching to inspire dramatic performance. David Garrick, eighteenth-century England's greatest actor, was also an outstanding director. He began by reading the script to the entire company, acting all the parts to clarify his goals. Next he talked about the play, mingling humour with specific commentary. As the actors took on their roles, he continually showed them how to achieve his interpretation, realistically assuming female as well as male behaviour as appropriate.

Garrick's coaching style invited the actors to copy him, which had its limitations. Modern coaching is more about enabling individuals to find their own way to be outstanding. But there will always be a place for the 'get up and show me what you mean' contribution.

The relationship between a theatre director and an actor offers business some useful tools for improving performance. For instance, to bring out the actor's best possible performance, the good theatre director needs creative collaboration: agreeing goals and having a deadline. At the heart of this lies a working partnership to devise something special. That is precisely how you can approach coaching in business, rather than merely instructing subordinates what to do.

Theatre-based coaching combines movement, text, voice and a visual element. In business we adapt it to offer a variety of creative techniques to release a person's potential, from visualization to improvisation, from rehearsal to role play. These lively sessions have a clear focus on shifting behaviour, since that is what improved performance is all about.

Coaches using a drama-based approach work with each person to become the author of their own production. There is no way of doing this except by being authentic. A theatre or film director works with the actor in that process, so that they can portray truthful aspects of themselves. Business leadership demands similar skills; it's just that the production doesn't happen in a theatre. In both cases the person being coached needs to be responsible for their own development.

QUICK COACHING

You can often coach somebody in five or ten minutes using the quick coach method. Simply support the person in exploring:

★   What is your objective? What do you want to achieve, what's the ideal outcome?

★   What's in the way of you getting what you want? Is the obstacle in you, in others or in the situation?

★   What action could you take to overcome the obstacles? This is where you can contribute as the coach, brainstorming options and exploring them with the person.

Give notes

After rehearsals, run-throughs and performances, actors assemble for 'notes'. It's a decisive moment, when the director gives everyone feedback on their performance and deals with any problems they have encountered. This constant monitoring of performance and feedback ensures that all the company continue to work well together.

Alec Guinness recalled the inspiring feedback from director Richard Eyre. During the last days of rehearsing Alan Bennett's *Habeas Corpus*, said Guinness, 'He would scribble schoolmasterly notes to each member of the cast at the end of every run-through. It was so much to the point, imaginative and stylishly written, that I regret not having saved them for future reference or as an example of what the relationship between actor and director should be.'

Trevor Nunn, once artistic director of the UK's Royal Shakespeare Company and National Theatre as well as director of musicals such as *Cats* and *Les Miserables*, gives continual feedback, always in a tactful, discreet fashion. Often he takes an actor aside, places a friendly arm around their shoulders, and whispers quiet,

FORMAL APPRECIATION

Carefully planned feedback occasionally proves memorably cathartic. For instance, in a workshop for one of London's large hotels, the senior engineer was stunned to hear his colleagues' appreciation of his leadership and how his team delivered excellent results. He was visibly moved at such feedback, since normally people only dealt with him when something went wrong, such as a failure in the air conditioning, when he was forced into troubleshooting.

> 'How you run an organization without sometimes causing emotional bruises is beyond me. I believe the only rule is to be as truthful as possible. People never thank you for softening blows by lying.'
> Peter Hall, director

insightful words in their ear. On returning to the rest of the cast, the actor might receive a shared smile and the remark, 'Oh, you've been Trevored.'

In contrast, George Kaufman, who directed scores of plays including Peter Ustinov's *Romanoff and Juliet* and the Pulitzer Prize-winning *You Can't Take It With You*, was exceedingly sparing in how he coached his actors. His response to one actor when she questioned his behaviour was: 'You're supposed to be good. I'll tell you when you're not.'

All these examples illustrate the variety of means and styles of delivering feedback. Since it's such a risky business, with the possibility of demoralizing people, choosing the appropriate feedback requires great sensitivity. There certainly needs to be a contract or agreement before delivering feedback, and normally a relationship of trust.

In the film business some producers are notorious for the stream of memos they send to everyone concerned with the production, from the director to the lowest runner in their hierarchy. But if you try to micro-manage through notes, you will neither inspire nor get the best from your people. The point of notes is that they arrive when they are useful, not just because you like bombarding people with your views.

Enrol everyone

Achieving high levels of enrolment becomes more essential as organizations become more complex. Yet often silent apathy prevails. Nor can you expect to change this overnight. Leaders often tell us: 'I ask for ideas and suggestions at our meetings, but nobody says anything.' Exploring this further, we usually find that employees have plenty of opinions and ideas to contribute. However, having been ignored for so long they remain unconvinced that their contribution will be heard, let alone acted on.

Imagine the following comments from a leader of a small travel business addressing her team:

> LEADER: Right, post-mortem time! It's been a long, tough day, but now the exhibition's finished I just want to say how disappointed I am by your total lack of commitment. Frankly, it was disastrous. We paid a fortune to take that stand and some of us bust a gut to get it ready on time. Yet hardly any of you were around to help put it up, staff it or even sell to the punters. What on earth went wrong?
> *Silence.*
> LEADER: We all agreed we would pull together and do it!
> *Silence.*
> LEADER: We all agreed, didn't we?
> TEAM MEMBER: Well, no, not really.
> LEADER: What? But I remember saying 'This will only work if we all pull our fingers out and get on with it.'
> TEAM MEMBER: Yes, that's true.
> LEADER: And nobody said 'no'.
> TEAM MEMBER: Right. But nobody really said 'yes' either.
> LEADER: Why not?
> TEAM MEMBER: Well, it seemed to be your thing and you were going to do it no matter what any of us said. So I suppose I just didn't bother saying anything.
> *Grunting agreement from others in the team.*

ENROLLING OTHERS

The best organizational changes start with inspiring and enrolling the individuals involved. Yet it is easy to lose sight of this fundamental principle if you become enamoured with grand schemes and corporate strategies.

Employees respond more to actions than words. They want tangible evidence of a real desire for their contribution, rather than token compliance. To deliver this evidence convincingly, you may need to:

★ Communicate your purpose with conviction.
★ Say why you need someone's help.
★ Describe how people can personally affect the outcome.
★ Invite people to say what they need in order to feel involved.
★ Show how the end result will affect people.
★ Explain the likely consequences of not enrolling.

> 'Treat people as if they are what they ought to be, and you help them to become what they are capable of being.'
> Johann Wolfgang von Goethe, writer

Leaders who claim that their people are disinterested in being involved may well be correct. They have made it become true because they so strongly believe it. For example, the newly appointed divisional head in one large company commented on how quiet his senior team meetings were. His group was responsible for 9,000 staff, so he depended on this team providing leadership. His predecessor had been an autocrat who encouraged empires, fiefdoms, divide and rule, and seldom wanted teamworking. The newcomer therefore started encouraging people to share ideas and opinions, taking care that they realized he was listening and acting on their ideas. It took time, but soon the floodgates opened and there was no stopping the team's latent energy.

If people can be part of creating their own future, they are more likely to 'own' it and thus feel involved and ultimately inspired. If conducted with flair, awaydays and planning events can

be great opportunities for promoting this process. The time taken
is a sound investment in enrolment, gaining commitment and giving people a chance jointly to create an inspiring future.

PLOTTING EVENTS

Awaydays to involve people in the planning process can be fun and highly creative. This is where you address such issues as:

★   What does outstanding performance look like?
★   What problems do we have to overcome?
★   What can stop us?
★   What can help us to go faster or be more efficient?
★   How do we improve communication?
★   What do people want to know?
★   What kind of organization do we need?
★   How do we keep our customers thrilled?
★   What are we missing?

We often become involved in making these strategic planning sessions more engaging. Many of our clients will run events that include such aspects as:

★   Exhibitions using craft materials and props to illustrate their solutions to current company challenges.
★   Creative presentations of the results of their planning.
★   Performances of adverts selling their ideas to others, including 'before and after' scenarios.
★   Acting sketches showing the benefits of strategic solutions, complete with props, hats and costumes.
★   The front page of future newspapers featuring headlines of what's happened over the past few years.

★   Television interviews with the leaders of the future reflecting on how they reached their current success.

In all cases, such processes help people embody their ideas so that they don't remain mere mind games. They also have a huge amount of fun developing the ideas and are therefore more likely to be involved in realizing these plans.

It is important only to use techniques appropriate to people's characters and levels of risk tolerance. There is nothing worse than pushing individuals into some sort of highly creative exercise if they view it as silly and embarrassing. In our experience, however, many groups find events that include this creative dimension enlivening and meaningful.

It is also important to build in good follow-through based on commitment to action by individuals and groups. Sometimes we encourage participants to write themselves post-dated letters or emails to provide reminders and encouragement.

These kinds of events can be highly effective at enrolling people in new plans and in solving seemingly intractable team or corporate issues.

SCENE 3
ORGANIZATIONAL INITIATIVE

During the scene change:

EXECUTIVE: I'll tell you what worries me. All this talk about making space to think creative and inspirational thoughts. And all this stuff about developing people. Where's the time?

PRODUCER: What time?

EXECUTIVE: You need time to plan and make sure everyone's with you – how's anyone going to get any work done?

PRODUCER: Time well spent, surely?

EXECUTIVE: It may be good practice, but my outfit expects delivery. We're totally results driven. We go faster and faster, the pace is relentless.

PRODUCER: It's the same in my business. The show must go on, remember? We've got paying customers too. In the theatre there's no place to hide. Your name's up there in lights, you're on stage, there's no choice, you must deliver.

EXECUTIVE: I agree there's got to be a real sense of urgency, and anyway I'm impatient by nature.

PRODUCER: All the best theatre directors I know are equally impatient. They're initiators, they make things happen. It's what makes them outstanding leaders.

The theatre's prime goal is performance. Everyone's there to get the show up and running. Actors literally take action and this defines their purpose – to act. The theatre is entirely action minded and this includes even the first day of rehearsals. Actors arrive anxious to get the play on its feet. Most of them will be wary of anyone who talks too much or directors who intellectualize about the drama. Their joint aim is to embody words in action.

For example John Dexter, a director at the UK's National Theatre and on Broadway, simply hated extensive discussions. Incredibly tough on his actors, he constantly sought human responses, not intellectual ones. He would demand: 'Don't tell me, show me!'

It was similar for Jack Lemmon working with director Billy Wilder for the first time on *Some Like It Hot*:

LEMMON: Billy, I've got an idea about this scene.
WILDER: Jack, don't ever tell me, 'cos I might
        misinterpret it totally. Do it, and let me see it.

Lemmon claimed: 'That's all you can ask of a director – that they let you try it. No matter how insane an idea it may be, they should let you try it.'

The wish to 'try it' recalls Judy Garland and Micky Rooney in their 1940s film musicals. At some telling moment in the story, the pair would utter the perennial showbiz call to arms: 'Let's do the show right here.' Though an oft-mocked cliché, it still conveys the enthusiasm, immediacy and action focus that we expect of artistic performances, as we saw earlier.

In business too this aliveness and 'in the moment' attitude can dramatically affect other people's performance. To get something special from your people, don't just talk about it, get on with it. There is an amazing difference in energy when people start implementing decisions. In meetings, once people are committed to an action, they can turn it straight into a diary appointment or put it on a 'to do' list. This gives it urgency and directness. Even better is when people can take action there and then: 'I'll make that call immediately; I'll sort the storeroom out right now; I'll make sure we send the letter off by lunchtime; I'll stay tonight until the project gets finished.'

Stage performers can become so wedded to the notion that the show must go on that they may even risk life and limb. For

'I want to be trusted. I want to be left alone to screw it up before they fix it or modify it or make it better.'
Julia Roberts, actor

instance, in the 1977 Broadway production of *The Gin Game*, actor Hume Cronyn continued playing despite a raging temperature. His wife Jessica Tandy, while consumed with anxiety, was equally keen to persist. Finally, director Mike Nichols suspended performances 'to save my stars from death by professionalism'.

Converting vision into reality is the toughest test for any leader, in the theatre or business. People will only support you because they want to be part of your adventure. If you are to claim their outstanding performance you must initiate and demand action, lead by example, set clear goals and persevere. Not much to ask!

> 'Never mistake motion for action.'
>
> Ernest Hemingway, writer

Demand action

> MANAGER: You've got to help me, it's an emergency.
>
> HEAD OF LEGAL SERVICES (HLS): What's the problem this time?
>
> MANAGER: One of my staff is utterly useless. I've just got to get rid of him.
>
> HLS: So what has he done?
>
> MANAGER: What he always does. He's a waste of space, with the intelligence of primitive pond life, and so annoying. You've got to help me make him redundant. What do I do?
>
> HLS: Is it something he's done recently or has this been going on for some time?
>
> MANAGER: For ever. From the moment he walked in the building he's been incompetent. I've always thought it and now he's proved it again.
>
> HLS: Fine. So how long exactly has he been with you?
>
> MANAGER: Umm... Fifteen years.

When clarifying our own company's core values, we realized it was important for us to make a real difference. While that might seem entirely obvious, we often meet leaders who are apparently intent on avoiding making such an impact. They are going through the motions, making the right noises about wanting change, yet they really have no stomach for it.

As a business leader or practising manager, most of the action you precipitate will be through the decisions you take. Being decision minded is perhaps easier in the theatre, because the constant tight deadlines towards the opening night force directors to make choices. Making decisions becomes a habitual part of the job. In the traditional corporate world the image of a manager wandering the corridors with a sheaf of papers in order to look busy can still prove a distraction.

Some good practice that encourages dynamic decision making needs to become part of your everyday leadership. For instance, notice the purpose of conversations. What are they really about? Do they explore ideas, create solutions, make decisions or simply promote gossip? How many of your conversations never lead to any action, or even a formal decision not to take action? Are your meeting minutes full of descriptions of what people talked about, rather than what they agreed to do and by when?

We are not arguing that every discussion must provoke a decision, only that it should be purposeful. This is why actors get so frustrated when working with directors who talk a lot in rehearsals. While discussion is valuable, the performers still have to turn it into action. And rehearsals should be totally focused on the impending performance.

It might be worth remembering some other simple good practice. We know this is obvious to many leaders, but it helps to set goals habitually and ensure accountability for delivery. We still work with senior managers who complain that their people simply will not take ownership of their actions. Or others who send their people off to implement initiatives and then don't monitor their progress over time. These basics are fundamental to delivering dramatic performance.

'I'd like to be a procrastinator, but I never seem to get round to it.'
Chris Dundee, humourist

GET ARCI

Some major corporations use sophisticated models such as Six Sigma to provide a framework that drives action in major projects. A rather simpler but equally effective approach is to get ARCI.

Every well-run project has someone who is accountable (A); that is, the decision maker. Others are responsible (R) for delivering results by an agreed date. During this process, some people need to be consulted (C). And yet others merely informed (I).

After any decision, try the discipline of drawing up a quick ARCI chart to ensure that it will happen. And of course, next to each person's name you must add a deadline. For example:

List the area of responsibility down the left-hand column, and then the people involved where it says X, Y, Z etc.

Under each person's name, identify who is accountable, responsible, being consulted and being informed.

A	Accountable
R	Responsible
C	Consulted
I	Informed

AREA	X	Y	Z		

GET SMART

SMART is a favourite mnemonic widely used for setting goals. Traditionally you set goals that are:

★ Specific
★ Measurable
★ Accountable
★ Recorded
★ Time limited

While this can encourage conventional performance, it hardly raises anyone's game or inspires them to excel.

Try changing the S to 'Stretching', which immediately alters the nature of the aim and encourages striving for dramatic performance. A stretching goal provides an exciting challenge and preserves the momentum towards excellence.

Create exciting performance goals

Old-style managers set goals and impose them on people, regardless of the reaction. That method of creating outstanding performance is in retreat in the face of complexity, talent shortages and people's increasing resistance to merely following orders. Even the armed forces have been finding that they need to adapt their approach.

Let people surprise you! Given the freedom, most will set far more demanding goals for themselves than any leader would willingly impose. However, this only works when you invest time in helping them stand back from day-to-day pressures to see the situation more clearly. Support them through coaching, awaydays, informal team discussions, mentoring, sabbaticals or simply allowing them time away from their desks to think.

Theatre directors adopt strict rehearsal schedules with fixed dates for run-throughs and technical rehearsals. They use these to set stretching goals for everyone involved, such as demanding that parts of the scenery are built and available to rehearse on, or costumes ready for a run-through prior to production week. Although they rarely sit down with actors and set performance targets as we know them in business, they will establish goals such as 'we need to have lines learnt for the next run-through'.

Setting conventional performance targets would be inappropriate in this situation. That is partly because qualitative brilliance is impossible to quantify, and also because the process is organic, so mechanistic goals would get in the way. You simply cannot plan for artistic breakthroughs. That's why good theatre needs a collaborative partnership between director and actor, where both people are working on identifying and agreeing the goals.

This approach of guiding someone towards a stretching goal is just as relevant in business. It demands an enabling leadership style so that people feel supported and yet challenged.

Persevere

However, there's a fine line between seeing things through and holding on too long. While you've got to show complete determination to get results; if you involve others you've also got to give them their head to see it through to the end. Experience tells us when to hold on, when to let go and when to give others free rein.

This is rather like the difference between 'delegating' and 'dumping'. Good delegation is a two-way process, negotiating with the person over whether they're capable and ready to take on a task or responsibility, setting some goals and coaching them through the process so that they're able to deliver what you want. Dumping is merely offloading onto someone with no support or choice.

Our capitalist society is meant to hunger for new ideas and supposedly stimulates breakthroughs and welcomes them with open arms. Yet history shows otherwise. In fact it often takes almost superhuman perseverance to win through, to make something you want happen. A perennial loser called Sparky, who had his cartoons rejected by the school magazine and even worse by Walt Disney, eventually turned himself into Schultz of Peanuts and Charlie Brown fame. Richard Attenborough took over a decade to get his film *Gandhi* into production. Five publishers turned down the Harry Potter books. James Dyson hawked his new style vacuum cleaner fruitlessly around scores of companies.

How come some people beat the odds? Is it luck, who they know, money, influence? Though all of these play a part, the main reason a new initiative wins is persistence. Someone, or maybe a whole team, takes responsibility for seeing it through. Such persistence usually stems from what is at stake.

Listen to Michael Attenborough about his directorial work at the Royal Shakespeare Company: 'I suppose the thing that people don't understand is the scale of responsibility. Everything, absolutely everything, is my responsibility. If a prop is wrong, if a costume doesn't look right, if a performance isn't happening correctly, if a lighting cue looks ridiculous – whatever – it's my responsibility, and I wouldn't have it any other way, speaking personally. It's very difficult in any walk of life (and certainly in artistic terms) to have partial responsibility for something, and the hallmark of the director's job is to take complete responsibility.'

For Harrison Ford it was his unshakeable inner belief in his ability that was at stake. Having trained as an actor he kept going for years, working in menial jobs and then as a carpenter on a film set, until he was finally picked for a prime film role.

Most actors know the humiliation of pitching for business in dispiriting auditions where they are treated like cattle. For them rejection is personal; it is not the same as having your product or

'It takes 20 years to make an overnight success.'
Eddie Cantor, performer

service turned down. Such experiences make performers experts in rejection that many of us would probably find intolerable. How they handle such struggle and persist carries important lessons for anyone in business aspiring to make things happen.

While persistence underpins all initiatives, it can also descend into irrational pig-headedness. That can happen to even the most talented person. To avoid it you need to be able to listen to those around you.

For actors and stage directors it's the audience who give you the warning. In business, the audience may be anyone from shareholders to employees who, like you, also care about the company. For example, against all advice, often passionately expressed, Lord Simpson of Marconi pressed ahead and sold the company's most pedestrian yet profitable lines of business. The company's shares became almost worthless within a year.

> 'Diamonds are only chunks of coal, that stuck to their jobs, you see.'
> Minnie Richard Smith, poet

Model the way

Actor Tommy Lee Jones appeared on Broadway with the more experienced performer Zero Mostel. When he wasn't performing Jones would stand in the wings studying Mostel: 'I couldn't take my eyes off him – I watched his every move.' Cast members often watch and learn from other leading players.

Sam Mendes, starting rehearsals for his Oscar-winning film *American Beauty*, asked the cast to use their personal experiences to affect their performance. Rather than telling them what to do, he led the way by being open about his own life. 'Such personal disclosure,' says actor Kevin Spacey, 'inspired the whole cast to bring an honesty to the process.' Mendes was modelling what he wanted others to do.

Senior company executives are likewise 'leading actors', highly visible and a focus of attention in times of change. There is constant pressure to practise what you preach. People watch you.

> 'I come from a profession where there was a lot of discipline. And because there was a lot of rejection you have to build a great deal of self-belief.'
> Christopher Reeve, actor, on coping with disability

STICKING WITH IT IN THE FACE OF REJECTION

If you need to persevere despite feeling that the world is against you, try some of the following tips:

★ Keep it in perspective. It might seem like the end of the world, but it isn't.
★ Get a good support structure of colleagues and friends to share the disappointment.
★ Keep practising so that you are not dependent on acceptance to exercise your craft.
★ Collect nos. If past experience tells you that you'll get ten nos for every yes, every no you receive is one nearer to a yes.
★ Don't take it personally. Remember, if you've been successful before, you can be again.
★ Set yourself review dates, when you take stock and recommit to your goals or decide to change them. This stops you feeling you are sticking with things indefinitely.
★ Make sure you build rejection into the process of whatever you're trying to achieve. It's an essential part of your plans.
★ Use rejection as a learning opportunity.

They measure their own performance against the standards you set. How you behave determines how they behave. You model the way.

Staff at Safeway's St Katharine's Dock grocery store in London tended to remove their personalities when they put on their uniforms. Encouraged to start behaving differently, they began taking the risk after seeing their managers behaving in new, more creative and outgoing ways. As Sue Scoular Davison, the company's training manager, put it: 'If the store management were prepared to shake out, sing and on occasions make fools of themselves, all in the spirit of fun and enjoyment, then so could everyone else.'

People want deeds not words. For example, on one of our development workshops, a group of senior bank managers at

ROLE MODEL

If you want others to change, first change yourself. This has long been the most effective way for skilful leaders to make important things happen in their organizations. Rather than demanding a personality transplant, it means becoming an effective role model.

Role models show the way through their behaviour and avoid mixed messages. And when you inevitably fall short, it implies that you come clean. For example, you might say to your team: 'Look, I don't mean to behave like that and I'm trying to change. So call me on it whenever you feel I'm not I practising what I preach. It's the only way I'll learn.'

Clarify the desired behaviour and actively communicate it. That way you will avoid saying one thing and doing another. Become accountable by inviting feedback. For example, is there an aspect of your own behaviour that you're working on and where it would be helpful to have support? By inviting this, you make yourself vulnerable, demonstrating a willingness to change and a personal commitment to development and outstanding performance.

Barclays discussed the future quality of their presentations. They all decided that they wanted to be 'as good at presenting as our CEO Matt Barrett'. Talented people want to be around leaders whom they can emulate and admire.

Like the star of any show, as a business leader you have few places to hide. You are always on stage and the spotlight usually finds you. Whatever personal difficulties this creates, it offers opportunities to influence the culture of the organization because people want to be led by example. It's an indirect way of coaching and mentoring.

Let your enthusiasm show

For theatre people, enthusiasm is an essential quality to help them keep going in adverse circumstances. It is like a glowing spark welling up from deep inside a person. It clearly contributes to their energy, and is also a vital part of inspirational leadership.

Too many workplaces seem devoid of enthusiasm, let alone the passion we discussed earlier. No wonder it is so hard in such companies to persist through all the obstacles. How can creativity thrive, new ideas flourish and people take risks when nobody seems to care much about what they are doing?

Our experience of working with senior management teams is that many of their difficulties come down to the missing ingredient of enthusiasm. Once they had in spades, now they have lost it, perhaps ground down by daily pressures or the bureaucracy of the enterprise.

Anything started with genuine, openly shared enthusiasm tends to create a buzz of excitement. It enlivens other people, even while it is enlivening you. Enthusiasm is not just nice to have, it is essential for promoting initiatives because it generates energy, builds commitment, encourages creativity and raises expectations.

So where does it come from? For example, does it entirely depend on your personality or can anyone have it?

Theatre professionals who have to keep going for months in long-running shows also risk losing their initial enthusiasm. However, this danger is taken seriously. The best directors build in numerous ways to get people back in touch with how they felt originally.

Actor Peter Barkworth talked about how he helped to sustain enthusiasm in a long West End run. 'I was in Michael Frayn's play *Donkey's Years* at the Globe Theatre. At every performance I gave an eight-minute party in my dressing room. All the actors, except for Penelope Keith and Andrew Robertson, who had an eight-minute scene in the middle of Act 2, used to come in, in their dinner jackets, and drink Perrier water and talk: we would discuss how the play was going at that performance, and what the audience was like; we would give each other occasional notes and generally

> 'I think enthusiasm rubs off on people, like pollen on bees.'
> Terence Conran, designer

chew the fat about plays, actors, directors, critics, authors and impresarios. Occasionally we would play round-robin games: What is the compliment you most like to receive a) as an actor b) as a person? Another was: What advice given by other people has most helped you?'

In working with teams we use similar processes in order to help people rediscover their enthusiasm. It is rewarding work, watching people get back in touch with their passion and desire for their work. Or seeing a group that was slumped and disconsolate unbend and, like a thirsty plant drinking in water, start to flower again.

Sometimes the enthusiasm is buried deep and when it finally comes to the surface there may be tears or great sadness. At other times it is like a sudden earthquake, when people explode into life with so much power and energy that they astonish and delight themselves.

There was a grumpy, gnarled and cynical engineer who taught people how to bore engine blocks in a UK-based car factory. Perhaps the very nature of his job had finally got to him, for he had sadly turned into a bit of a bore himself. 'All a load of bollocks,' he grumbled at the start of our workshop.

At first he sat there glowering, his large hands placed rather delicately on his knees. The other participants did their best to encourage him, but he was having none of it.

This workshop, appropriately called Dramatic Shift, used theatre techniques to break through resistance to change and build a willingness to make new things happen. But our engineer was apparently unable to play, until something shifted when he was asked to re-enact scenes from his earlier life. He began talking of the energy and enthusiasm he had possessed in abundance when starting work at the company two decades earlier. He started loosening up when asked to turn a blank white mask into a vivid expression of how he felt about working in the company.

Then came the big moment. On stage, people were asked to put on their newly painted masks and to walk around conveying the emotion of the mask. Our engineer hesitated, then, looking slightly abashed, even puzzled to find himself doing it, he slipped on the mask. Safely hidden behind the mask, he began walking around the room with everyone else, behaving in ways that would certainly have astounded his friends. The mask had freed him up to face new possibilities as well as old truths.

This burnt-out man who had entered the room so resistant to much that was on offer stood more erect, walked with vigour and even laughed out loud. And later, when on stage again performing a speech from a play that he had found inspiring, he got back into contact with what he had lost and began reviving a long-extinct enthusiasm. He had simply become worn down by the organization and had forgotten that he was a naturally enthusiastic human being, able to have a positive effect on those around him. Talking about the experience, he appeared moved and gratified at reawakening an important part of himself. In doing so, he moved everyone else in the workshop. Now, at last, he saw what he had lost and part of him was both sad and angry.

He announced that he was determined to work in a different way. He even took this new-found enthusiasm home that night, returning the next day to describe how he had announced to his startled family: 'I'm sick and tired of being a boring old fart. Things are going to change.' And they did. This had a profound and enlivening impact on his family, for such vitality can indeed be inspirational.

Theatrical methods offer a useful technology for enabling leaders to reinvigorate themselves. Yet maybe all it takes is giving people a chance to rediscover themselves, to remember how they used to be when younger. Sometimes people have simply lost touch with their natural vitality.

Keep it fresh

Actor Anthony Sher once received a painful and unexpected kick up the backside from fellow actor Jonathan Pryce during a performance on stage. Sher recalls, 'The kick said: "wake up", it said, "you're on automatic, you're just doing what you've done before". It was a rough lesson but a good one.' He added, 'It's essential to reinvent, re-mint each moment in a play again and again, night after night.' As with life, drama is spontaneous and risky: 'There are certain scenes of crisis and emergency when real danger is required, something you can't fake. The actor has to send a frightening jolt through the air, surprising the audience, surprising the other actors, surprising himself.'

So how do you keep alive the whole process of initiating change in your company? The danger is that once it is underway it can become repetitive and dull, just like any long-running theatre production (see the box overleaf). As an actor, Michael Maynard had two contrasting experiences illuminating this issue. The first was playing in a pantomime for three months. 'By the middle of February the show had turned sour, not just because we were still asking audiences to sing along to Christmas songs or invite Santa to their party. We also faced no challenge, no danger and no risk. We were going through the motions and doing silly things to keep us awake. It was predictable, safe and boring.'

Performing in an even longer-running national tour of a Mike Leigh play was entirely different. The best performance the cast gave was on the 100th show, six months after the opening. By then the whole company had grown and developed and people simply got better and better. By the end of the tour each performance was like a first night; which of course it was for the audience.

These two experiences show the difference between dead and alive theatre. In one the cast were sleepwalking through their performance, in the other they were entirely awake. How many companies have performers who are similarly sleepwalking through the day?

Michael MacLiammoir, an actor/director, comments: 'We are born at the rise of the curtain and we die with its fall and every night in the presence of our patrons we write our new creation. And every night it is blotted out forever. And of what use is it to say to audience or to critic: "Ah, but you should have seen me last Tuesday"?'

'Surprise yourself with your own daring.'
Laurence Olivier, actor

A large UK leisure company owns several holiday villages through the country. On every site there are sales people whose job it is to sell people caravans or get them to upgrade their current holiday home. Over the years the company has devised a sales pitch and its people are trained in how to deliver the script. The difficulty is that as time goes on, the members of the sales team become mechanical in the way they deliver the message. Saying the same things over and over again means that they tend to go onto auto-pilot and lose sight of the individuality of each customer.

Exploring the issue in a drama-based workshop not only encouraged the 'performers' to adjust their delivery according to the people they were talking to, it also produced two other key improvements. One focused on the actor's skill of delivering repetitive information and keeping it fresh. We call this the 'Mousetrap syndrome' after the long-running Agatha Christie play. Actors face this challenge performing night after night in the same play. It involves a level of concentration to recreate the material afresh each time and an absolute focus on the audience, for whom this is a first night. The second key technique from which the sales people benefited was the notion that the more they are involved in creating the script in the first place, and the more freedom they have to improvise, the less like zombies they become. This was a challenge to senior management, who had to trust their people rather than control them. The outcome, however, produced instant benefits when there was a revived twinkle in the eyes of those delivering what had previously been a dead script.

What sort of theatre of change will you create? Will it be exciting, vibrant and full of initiative, even danger, so that it attracts talent? Or will it be a tired revival, a safe, mediocre drama that should never have seen daylight? It's a real distinction. Though it is hard to define, employees, just like audiences, know instinctively when they are being invited to be part of something worthwhile.

Dramatic success occurs when people are free to take the initiative and make things happen. To keep the process alive, people need to feel that they have the power and responsibility to react to changing circumstances. For actors, those changing

AVOID TICK BOXES

The 'tick boxes' approach to management is the equivalent of 'going through the motions' in a theatre performance. It is done for all the right reasons, mainly to standardize excellence in particular areas. Sadly, it often produces the exact opposite.

Take a sales assistant in a complaints department who followed the procedures for producing outstanding customer service, as laid down in the 'rulebook'. He ticked all the right boxes to show that the job was done properly:

★   Have you said your name and the name of the company?
★   Have you got their name and details?
★   Did you listen accurately to their complaint?
★   Did you acknowledge the complaint and repeat a summary back to the customer to demonstrate that you have heard it accurately?
★   Did you ask what the customer thinks they deserve by way of recompense?

However, he omitted a crucial factor. He forgot to think about what he could personally do that would make it special for the customer. So instead of delivering anything like outstanding service, he could only provide something that was competent. He became an automaton, lacking the human contribution that is the key to outstanding customer service. He may have produced service according to the book, but it failed to make an impression as anything special, which was the whole point of the exercise.

There are many areas where this tick boxes approach is pursued, everywhere from call centres and helplines to appraisals. People are ticking boxes for the approved behaviour and in the process missing out any possible personal initiative. It is the equivalent of a troupe of actors working their way through a performance ticking off the scenes as they go: 'That's scene six done, now on to scene seven...' Hardly a recipe for magic.

A large hierarchical UK company in the financial sector was grappling with two problems. On the one hand, the members of the senior team were overwhelmed with work and responsibility. On the other, the people below them were complaining about not having enough power and responsibility. The company solved both problems in one fell swoop. It simply moved everything, throughout the company, down a level.

Whatever the decision-making authority and budget-holding power were at one level in the organization, it was extended to the next management level down. Instead of the senior team controlling everything, its direct reports were empowered to take the relevant initiatives. They weren't asked to refer everything upwards for approval. Instead, they were trusted to take appropriate decisions.

This process was replicated throughout the company. It sent a tangible message of trust throughout the organization, and also lightened the burden of the senior management and speeded up the working of the company as a whole.

circumstances normally involve the audience in some way. In most organizations it is customers, both external and internal. By focusing on their individuality and unique needs, you can stay fresh and excited even if you and your staff are performing repetitive roles.

Share the action

'If you give an audience a chance, they will do half your acting for you.'
Katharine Hepburn, actor

There is a dilemma facing many organizations. Do we need stars or teamwork? Shall we reward individual effort or the group? Must the star always hog the limelight or is there room for anyone else?

Initiative in organizations depends on sharing the action. For example, Microsoft saw how Xerox's renowned research facility did brilliant work, yet this never permeated the rest of the company. Learning the lesson, Microsoft moved its entire research arm into its headquarters, making sure that product managers constantly talked about the numerous research initiatives. It even sponsored an internal fair in which those with new ideas could bid for attention from people around the company. Over 20,000 people attended.

If you want to get your organization's act together, don't hog the limelight. You need a culture where everyone can take initiative. Sounds messy? Of course, but then who said being creative, persistent and enthusiastic happens in any other way? In fact, the evidence is that effective leadership of a team or a whole company tends to move around. Companies that have got their act together create a theatre in which there are constant rewards and recognition for all kinds of people who push for action; likewise for people who take responsibility and exercise it wisely.

To transform your company situation requires not merely this kind of leadership, but also knowing both where to start and when. Before you can begin making changes, you need to possess a thorough understanding of your current drama and have a picture of what the future would look like.

Take a look at your current daily drama

Seeing your organization afresh when you are so used to the everyday activity can be difficult. Viewing your organization like a stage play may sound odd, yet it's a powerful and creative way of getting a new perspective on what's going on around you. Here is how people in various companies we have worked with described their particular drama:

★ It's like *Carry On Cowboy*, with all the senior managers running around and shooting themselves in the foot.

★ It's like a French farce, characters rushing about avoiding each other, total chaos and probably lots of hanky-panky going on, which would explain some of the odd promotions.

★ It's like *Titanic*: we've passed the stage of rearranging the deck-chairs, now the ship's sinking and everyone's fighting over the lifeboats.

★ It's like *Star Trek*, with all our consultants out there at Warp Factor 9, boldly going where no one has boldly gone before, and I'm in the engine room shouting 'We dinna have the power, captain!' It's business, Jim, but not as we know it.

Now that you are standing outside of the drama, the big question is do you really want to be part of it? Perhaps there are bits that excite you; otherwise, you probably wouldn't still be working there. Yet many people regard their organizations as tawdry productions, staggering on with poorly trained casts that have long since lost sight of the plot. Even if yours is fine, probably many aspects could be improved. There's a lot you can do, but first you need to clarify where to put your attention.

Create a compelling drama for the future

What do you want the future to look like? It's like writing a script for a play: what exactly will it say and describe? What sort of drama will you create to attract and retain the best talent? For that you need some kind of vision.

Some of the busiest and most profitable consultancies in recent years have been those helping business to develop a vision for the future and advising on how to create it. Yet most of the lofty pronouncements and elaborate strategic techniques can ultimately be reduced to what we call 'the script'; that is, the story or mental picture that people have in mind of how the business might look.

Writing this script is simpler than many experts in strategy and vision would have us believe. While you do need imagination, it is generally equivalent to walking round an apartment that you might rent. As you go from room to room you imagine how the place would look if you made some changes. Vision is really just an imagined future that is an improvement on the present.

CURRENT EVERYDAY DRAMA

Imagine you are sitting in a theatre auditorium. On stage is a play depicting your working life. It's all up there: the people you work with, the spotlight on the organization, the drama of everyday existence.

An actor plays you as you come and go. What is this play really about and what is actually going on? What is the plot and who are the key characters? Like all good dramas, there is normally a sub-plot, plenty of things happening beneath the surface ready to emerge later and provide the excitement as the drama reaches its climax.

Plays are written in different styles. There are thrillers and melodramas, comedies and farces, epic tragedies, domestic kitchen-sink dramas and surreal fantasies. What is the style of this particular piece that you are seeing on stage in your imagination? What is the likely outcome and how do you think the plot will develop?

The only envisioning that will make an impact in the real world is one that excites you personally. This is why so many business strategies, carefully devised, meticulously researched and documented, nevertheless end up as lost causes. Somehow they don't set people on fire, no one gets excited and they arouse no passion.

To produce something that gets your juices flowing, a script that comes alive on your corporate stage, you may need to dig deep to discover your own passions, your vision for yourself and your future, as we have already discussed. Nor does this have to come just from you. It is often far more effective as a shared task between those who really care about the company's future. Much of our own work in this area is not so much about strategy as helping people discover what hits the right buttons, raises energy levels and taps into their wish to create something extraordinary, rather than pedestrian.

When you become clear on a vision for yourself, you achieve more than a selfish look at the future. It is not mere navel gazing, since the results can be profound. Personal reflections can provide

'I don't know who writes the scripts, but they're amazing.'
David Beckham, footballer, on his World Cup experience

CLARIFYING YOUR PERSONAL ORGANIZATIONAL VISION

How you personally would like to see the future can come from reflecting on:

★ When have I felt most fulfilled at work?
★ When have I been most appreciated?
★ What would I like to exist in my working life in the near future that isn't present now?
★ What would I most like to happen in the coming year?
★ How would I like to be remembered?
★ When I look around my current situation, what is most needed?
★ What do I want most of all?
★ What could I do that would make the most difference to my working life?
★ What could I do that would make the most difference to other people's lives?
★ What would my ideal everyday working life look like if it were portrayed on stage?
★ Who else is involved?

a firm base for taking a confident, wider view of how you want to transform your workplace.

So what is the production you want to create or be part of? Even if you are unable to direct the entire company's performance, you can at least start to devise a script for how you would like your area of work to be, whether it's a team, a department or a division.

In theatre, the playwright usually writes down the script to provide guidance to the performers on what their vision is. Even when actors mainly improvise, they often record the results so they can refer to them later. Before your business actors get to work, you need to refine the script into something dramatic that truly inspires people.

When you share the vision with others it has to engage hearts and minds. Being excited yourself is a big step, but it may not be

SHORT STORY

'High concept' is Hollywood's shorthand for reducing the story of a potential film so that it can be communicated in a few memorable phrases. They might say, for example, that it's a bit like…

★   *Wuthering Heights* in space.
★   Boy meets girl who guesses lottery numbers correctly and both nearly get killed for them.
★   Man walks across the US and people start seeing him as a guru.
★   *Thelma and Louise* meets *The Shawshank Redemption*, a feel-good prison drama.
★   A woman stumbles across a manuscript and sells it as her own, only to find that it's a forgery.

Compelling stories and plays that make an impact have a strong core meaning and a dynamic narrative. They are not shaggy-dog stories, with people rambling on. Instead, the plot is refined and the point made with impact.

So what is your high concept story for your company? Can you sum up your vision for the future in a short phrase or sentence?

enough to get things moving when you convey your message. No matter how well constructed the script, people interpret the experience of watching it for themselves. You don't 'roll out' your organizational vision or transfer it through 'branding' it with wall charts or an internal advertising campaign.

You need a process that will:

★ Paint a picture, explain the future.
★ Convey your own passion, enthusiasm and commitment.
★ Demand evidence of sustained action.
★ Clarify the new behaviour that will be required.

★ Offer help to make the changes.

★ Make sense to each person from their unique perspective.

★ Manage expectations.

It's the job of the director, cast and crew to transform the script into a thrilling and entertaining experience. In business, too, leaders need to undertake a similar process if they are to produce the dramatic performance they envisage.

I know what I want to achieve. I now have a very clear picture of the sort of production I want to create in my part of the business. The issue for me now is: How do I go about making it happen?

There are two distinct issues here. One is about where to start – where you need to put your attention. And then it's about when to start – knowing the right time.

EXECUTIVE

PRODUCER

WHERE TO START

When Cameron Macintosh produced *Phantom of the Opera*, he was unsure that it would be a success right up until the dress rehearsal. It was only at that critical moment that he realized it was working. 'Its wonderful music, exciting staging, great cast – all the pieces of the clockwork came together. The look and the sound of the show were intertwined. It was an alchemy.'

Whether you want to improve the performance of a team, department, division or the whole company, the principle is the same. You can't just flick a few switches and expect it all to happen automatically. Remember, you are dealing with an organism, not an organization. Your part of the company is just like the rest of life: a dynamic, quivering rhythm of fluctuations and tension. Any change in the pulse can affect the whole. It is fluid and continually changing of its own accord, even without your intervention. So you need to view the process holistically and put your attention on the factors that will make the most difference.

Research in complexity science shows how relatively small changes in an organism can trigger unpredictable effects. This certainly applies to companies. While particular factors will produce change, it is unlikely that one or two alone will make a difference. It takes a combination of actions to achieve the shift.

Unlike in the theatre, where you can prepare a new set in advance and suddenly reveal it to the audience with a nifty scene change, your organizational shift is likely to be in full view of your audience. If you want to retain their interest, indeed even get them to take part in changing the scenery, you need to discover the 'touch points' in the culture and start working on them. Touch points make the difference between your vision merely being an aspiration and it becoming a reality in which people feel the difference and get excited and hungry to be part of the transformation.

So where do you start the process? There is an ongoing debate in the acting profession about how you go about building a character. Is it 'inside out' or 'outside in'? The actor Beryl Reid liked to get her stage character's shoes right. Once she knew how the person stood and walked, she could work the rest out. Sigourney Weaver was the same for her part in *Galaxy Quest*. She found the character's walk, or rather her 'glide', and the rest of the portrayal started from there. Alec Guinness felt similarly about the character's voice. On the other hand, many actors such as Daniel Day Lewis, Angelica Huston or Dustin Hoffman leave the externals till later. They assume that these will follow naturally if they first get the inner personality right.

> 'One obstacle always stopped me directing films – namely having to say "action". My instinct would be too say "Er, I think if everybody's agreeable we might as well sort of start now – that is if you're ready."'
> Alan Bennett, playwright

> 'It is clear that the future holds opportunities – it also holds pitfalls. The trick will be to seize the opportunities, avoid the pitfalls and get home by 6 pm.'
> Woody Allen, writer/director

DRAMATIC TOUCH POINTS

Hewlett-Packard UK identified seven 'touch points' as keys to changing culture. These included customer service, incentive schemes, environment, a 'can do' attitude and leadership. Taking each of these, the company devised a strategy for change. Each alone was insufficient; a holistic approach was required.

'Touch points' literally touch people in some way. For example, when HP staff arrived on Monday to find office layouts changed to incorporate lounge areas and colourful sofas, they realized that this was a serious initiative.

The various change initiatives also have to complement each other. In HP's case, the leadership development also needed to reflect the 'can do' attitude and the spirit of the new culture. Thus it came in various different forms, everything from coaching to conference events, from 360 degree feedback to workshops. These provided material used to affect the other touch points.

Other companies have identified their own dramatic touch points or critical factors for starting change and sustaining it: the IT system, decision-making process, management structure, dress code, budget-holding power, communication system, knowledge management, suggestion schemes, market awareness and performance reviews.

Identify the ones that will have the most dramatic effect and work on those first, while reinforcing them with the others over time.

Applied to our challenge to change your area of the organization, do you work from the 'outer theatre' inwards; that is, from the corporate to the individual level? Or do you work from the 'inner theatre' outwards; that is, from individual behaviour to the corporation? Both are viable since it is an organic process – an art, not mechanical engineering. In effect, both need to be worked on at the same time. The dramatic touch points are likely to include elements from both areas.

Get the right people

Ultimately it is people, with their commitment, energy and creativity, who transform companies. Often they do this in a fraction of the time required by elaborate change mechanisms. In simple terms, the more people oriented your business becomes, the more profitable it tends to be.

For example, dramatically improved performance seldom seems to stem from massive restructuring, reengineering, mergers or other mechanistic interventions. Even when these do affect change, the process can prove highly damaging and it can also take years for the results to show, by which time competitors have moved far ahead. Relying on these to change performance is like expecting a new lighting rig to create an ensemble, or a new safety curtain to improve a cast's performance.

It is more helpful to see companies as personalities in their own right, constantly adapting organisms consisting of a collection of individuals. Outstanding company performance comes from outstanding individual performance, usually within a team situation.

When your people feel that their talent is valued and at centre stage, they are more likely to contribute creatively to raising the levels of performance in the organization. When they feel sidelined, they do exactly the opposite. So in your production, ask yourself what it will take to engage the human spirit, the life force for delivering company effectiveness.

'I direct as little as possible. I relieve myself of the ardours of direction, simply by casting it right.'
John Huston, director

Focus on action and behaviour

It will definitely take a change in behaviour. But what behaviour will create the change you want? It can take weeks, months or more to identify, communicate, develop and begin rewarding new behaviour that will create a company's new 'drama', its script of the future. Nevertheless, there is no viable alternative to this essential work.

A favourite way in which companies try to affect employee behaviour and create corporate-wide change is through branding. These are large-scale communication programmes with all the trappings of high-powered marketing and PR.

Let's eavesdrop on how such an approach emerges for a possible culture change:

The scene: A group of creatives are meeting at A.G. Young, Young, Baker, Bart and Thompson, a London-based agency specializing in branding. Beers, sweets and crisps litter the expensive and fashionable clear glass table. In walks Jeremy, who handles the account for the Premier chain of hotels.

JEREMY: OK, you stars of the corporate firmament, time for your creative juices to flow. Premier are going upmarket, people. They're going to challenge Ian Shrager, Intercontinental *et al.* Comprende? We've designed the new brand for them so we know how it's all going to look. The ads are out there and the new decor is underway. But we have a teenyweeny problem.

AVRIL: No one told the staff?

JEREMY: Sadly so, my little cherub. They're all still behaving like they're some three-star standard bolthole, for God's sake. So they need to change. You know what that means. We want them to deliver total quality service. We've got to take these rather dull and stale people, shake them and get them living the logo!

GORDON: We've done this before, haven't we? No probs. Lots of town hall meetings to explain the brand concept, videos and wall charts, newsletters, handy pocket cards with the brand values on, email reminders, daily living the logo sessions. You know the sort of thing. Hey, we could even run a competition for staff on the benefits of the new brand to customers.

JEREMY: OK, that should do the trick. Let me have something by Friday.

These often elaborate and expensive branding exercises seldom cause actual behaviour change. They may briefly affect attitudes, but this is like raising consumer awareness of a new electric toothbrush without persuading people to buy it, change the habits of a lifetime and start using it twice a day.

For sustainable change, you need to do more than raise the brand image or start to shift attitudes. Nor is it enough to get people involved. They need to start practising the new forms of behaviour and receive encouragement when they demonstrate these. In turn, this poses a whole new set of challenges for those leading the change. Ideally, it is best if instead of simply selling a message – the branding approach – you involve people in identifying for themselves the new behaviour they will require to achieve the desired change.

> 'Acting is all about bringing the performance down to behaviour, behaviour, behaviour. People look, behave and react.'
> Michael Caine, actor

WHEN TO START

What's the compelling reason?

Ready or not, the curtain rises on opening night. This brutal reality concentrates everyone's minds, urging people to go that extra mile if necessary, even working through the night. It may take Herculean efforts to alter a theatrical production at the last minute so that against the odds the performance succeeds.

Corporations also need a compelling reason for initiating change. People must understand and feel the imperative for action. At the strategic level, the catalyst may include a threat to market share, relocation, a fall in equities, business upturns or downturns, increased competition, new legislation, a visioning process, a strategic initiative or a financial crisis. For business leaders the challenge is how to translate such situations into compelling reasons that will affect absolutely everyone in the organization.

For example, in a major hotel chain the leadership talked of 'the chambermaid effect', finding a compelling reason for the hotel cleaners to change their behaviour in response to a rebranding exercise that was taking the hotel service upmarket.

Who owns it?

SYLVIA: I have a great scheme for improving performance in this company. I reckon we could revolutionize our client relations system. That means not only getting a new contact management IT system, but also completely changing the way our people relate to customers. I want them to develop a completely new skill set. So I'm going to book a whole series of training courses to get things moving.

CONSULTANT: That all sounds great, but can I just check who else is behind this? Do you have the backing of senior management? Is it linked to the company's business plan? Do you have the budget to make it happen?

SYLVIA: Not really. It's just that I'm convinced it would make a difference. I suppose you could say I'm leading from the front.

CONSULTANT: Yes, but every now and then you need to look around and see if anyone is with you!

In our development work within companies, we push hard to unravel who has a stake in the change effort succeeding.

Surprisingly, the owner of the change effort often emerges as the human resources professional rather than the CEO or even other key senior leaders. These are really the accountable people whose jobs may be on the line if the change effort fails. Even when they are at board level, HR representatives seldom have enough leverage to make a major change effort stick. For example, they depend almost entirely on the willingness of line managers to promote new behaviour.

Gather energy

Watch the stage or film version of the high-powered show *Chicago* and you may well wonder where the performers get so much energy. Theatre groups galvanize and sustain enormous energy over long periods and have developed an impressive technology to achieve this repeatedly. This has useful lessons for business organizations.

Peter Hall's diary of his period at the UK's National Theatre, for example, reveals the enormous drive needed to keep productions going at the Old Vic theatre while wrestling with building work and its planners and architects. Similarly, one of the greatest examples of finding huge reserves of energy in order to persevere was Sam Wanamaker's epic journey of decades of fundraising to recreate Shakespeare's Globe theatre on London's South Bank. He was pursuing this dream while also working as a full-time actor.

It is an extremely fortunate leader who is given time off to dedicate themselves exclusively to driving a particular change initiative. On the whole, you still have to juggle all the existing plates as well as adding a new one to your act. This requires huge energy.

Energy may come from someone's personal vision, passion or personal investment. Or it may stem from crises that threaten the entire organization. For any change initiative to work, you will need to gather a committed team of people around you who are enthusiastic and persevering.

Keep it simple

Renowned investor Warren Buffett relies on simplicity to guide his important decisions: 'I never invest in anything I don't understand.' Or take Dianne Thompson, boss of UK lottery company Camelot: 'I have a very common-sense approach to business. I also have a can-do mentality; I always think there are solutions to be had.' Or as Charles Dunstone, chairman of Carphone Warehouse, puts it: 'I am surprised that other people are amazed at what we have done, because it's not particularly amazing. It's all applied common sense, what we do.'

Business is complicated enough without introducing a complicated approach to improving performance. In an era of specialists, for example, we receive a steady stream of esoteric solutions, to say nothing of theories, models and elaborate processes designed to create changed performance. Yet it is simplicity, not complexity, that usually brings the best results.

When Geest ended its fruit import business – in its own words, 'stopped being bananas' – conventional wisdom said the management had got it all wrong. But the company's young team relied on its own common sense to create an even more successful fresh food business.

We know many clients who have spent so long trying to work out what's best that they have missed that vital moment. This tends to occur through an over-reliance on reports, diagnostics, enquiries and surveys that ultimately only describe potential change. They are like menus in a restaurant describing the food. Don't eat the menu thinking that you're having a good meal! It's about action. And as performers say, it's all about timing.

A grand scheme

For people to support you in your vision, they need to feel part of something special. Theatre directors achieve this by creating a partnership with their actors, designers, stage managers and technicians. They also offer new perspectives, create an atmosphere of experimentation and interpret the play to bring it to life on stage. The best directors go further by seeking truthful and authentic performances of an outstanding quality, all within a commercial environment that is intolerant of failure.

'Today, we make everything so complicated. The lighting, the camera, the acting. It has taken me 30 years to arrive at simplicity.'
Sven Nykvist, cinematographer

Veronica Roberts is an experienced actor and a consultant at MLA. We asked her about her experiences of working with some renowned theatre directors and how they got the best out of the actors.

Of the famous Russian director Yuri Lyubimov, who directed a notable production of *Crime and Punishment*, she says: 'Trust was inevitably involved. A willingness to trust the man's vision. It was an endeavour in which the whole was bigger than any one ego contained within it. There was a conscious sacrifice of self to this company creation.' Veronica was nominated for Best Supporting Actress and the production won the UK Best Play award.

'Working with Mike Leigh also requires the actor to lay down any need to control and know all the time. Everyone works as hard as everyone else, as though they are going to be the star of the show. Flexibility, spontaneity, playfulness and a sense of adventure and willingness to enjoy the ride are essential. Enjoying the journey for it's own sake helps enormously.'

'With Mike Alfreds you start and end with the script. What is it? What does it mean? What are the facts? How can we interpret them? And essentially, how can one stay alive and alert in performance, minting it new and afresh every single evening?'

From these varied experiences she reflects on what produces outstanding performance: 'Something they all had in common for me is that they made it seem like a grand scheme to be part of. There would be no guarantees, but by God, it would be a thrill. They made it seem like a tightrope walk, an off-piste ski run, an abseil down Everest; something that one would feel *alive* about. Sometimes it felt almost mundane, like simply knowing one's function and being willing to fulfil it. But being valued for one's contribution along the way causes actors to give of themselves tirelessly and often in difficult circumstances, where sometimes they cannot see or comprehend what direction is being taken. Constant communication and giving bearings creates safety in freefall situations.'

You too will need to create a grand, exciting and important scheme if people are to feel inspired to be part of it. Only then will you transform your part of the organization and produce dramatic success.

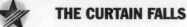

THE CURTAIN FALLS

THE PLOT SO FAR...

Act III explored the three critical leadership capabilities needed to transform your organization's performance:

★   Scene 1 – Organizational insight: how to understand your talent and see what's needed.

★   Scene 2 – Organizational inspiration: how to inspire and involve people.

★   Scene 3 – Organizational initiative: how to implement with a ruthless commitment to delivery.

To change your part of the business involves knowing:

★   Where to start – identifying the dramatic touch points for change.

★   When to start – how to get the timing and conditions right so as to maximize the chances of success.

Once again, we can go behind the scenes and see how people are implementing the ideas covered in Act III in their workplaces.

BEHIND THE SCENES

In which Dan gets some quick coaching

Jo: Come in, Dan. Looks like you need to talk.

Dan: I should have dropped in before. I thought I could sort this one out myself, but I need some help. It's the sales team, they're just not delivering.

Jo: Meaning?

Dan: Meaning they're fine implementing instructions, but we need more – a lot more.

Jo: You want them to be more proactive in contacting clients, to make things happen without being told what to do?

Dan: Exactly, you've got it.

Jo: Let's use my 'quick coach' approach on this one. You found it useful last time we tried it. First up, let's get clear what your objective is. Think six months from now. Ideally, what would it look like?

Dan: Well, there'll be a real buzz, a sense of energy about the place. You know, people creating leads, not just following them up.

Jo: Go on.

Dan: Ideally they would all be supporting each other with ideas on what they could do to make things happen, bring in more business.

Jo: So that's your objective. What about the obstacles?

Dan: I know, I know. Are they in the people, in the situation or…

Jo: Or in you?

Dan: Yes, I guess I'm a bit fed up with all this pushing and nagging I have to do. It's so wearing.

Jo: So that's you. What about the obstacles in other people?

Dan: They're so reactive! Of course they're under pressure and all that, but…

Jo: They could do more?

Dan: Right. I mean, it's easier just talking to clients they know than going out there and finding new ones. I'm not sure they even know how important that is right now.

JO: And what about the situation itself? Any blocks there?

DAN: That's easy. We need a much better database system. The stuff on clients isn't as good as it should be. And we don't have a good way of sharing knowledge between us.

JO: Got it. OK. We've got a clear objective. We've nailed down the obstacle, so now we...

DAN: Do the creative bit?

JO: You're ahead of me. Yep, now we look at possible actions. Let's start with you. You said you're fed up chasing people to perform, and besides you don't have the time.

DAN: And how. Anyway, it doesn't work, no matter how tough I get.

JO: So is there anyone else who might follow through on this for you?

DAN: Now you mention it, Natalie's been harping on about sharing knowledge for ages. Maybe I could ask her to lead on this and see where it goes from there.

JO: Good idea. What about the team's reluctance to make proactive calls? How could we encourage them to do that? Could it be a confidence issue?

DAN: In some ways, definitely. Hey, why don't we do some training and practise cold-calling techniques?

JO: Makes sense to me. Can you handle that yourself or do you need outside support on this?

DAN: I'll get in some nice pastries and stuff and we'll run some breakfast practice sessions. Let's have a go ourselves to start with.

JO: OK. See how you get on and let me know if you need some extra input. Now what about the situation, got any creative thoughts on that?

DAN: You're going to buy me a brand new, state-of-the-art contact management system?

JO: Not exactly, but I'll do some digging. Meanwhile, what about some incentives to reward people for sharing their knowledge?

DAN: You mean pay them to talk to each other?

JO: More like rewarding the team as a whole if they demonstrate sharing information and start performing as a unit.

DAN: That's neat, I like it. Why didn't I think of that?

Jo: You will next time! It might also solve some of the other issues you have.

DAN: Jo, this has really been helpful. Let me start writing down some of these actions we've discussed. At last I feel I'm making some progress here.

—··

Jo's dramatic coaching framework provides a quick route to supporting people in problem solving.

In order to make progress, Dan needed to:

★ Clarify his objective
★ Identify the obstacles:
   – in himself
   – in others
   – in the situation
★ Gain support in creating action to overcome each of the obstacle areas.

Jo gave swift support and became an active partner in the creative process.

—··

In which team members face their nightmare scenario

The production team of a food magazine is contemplating its situation.

TIM: I called us in early this morning for a hard look at our present situation.

GLORIA: What is it? Are people not buying magazines any more or what?

JACK: Maybe they're just not buying ours. Have we got any figures on the competition?

NICKY: No, they lie like we all do and pretend things are better.

TIM: Seriously, we've got to do something.

GLORIA: Well, it can't get any worse.

TIM: Maybe it could.

JACK: What do you mean?

TIM: I really think we should consider a worst-case scenario.

JACK: A collective nightmare – what fun!

GLORIA: OK. People get completely fed up with magazines.

NICKY: Or with food magazines especially.

JACK: Nobody buys a magazine at all, ever.

GLORIA: If they buy any magazine, they buy somebody else's or...

JACK AND GLORIA: They go on the internet!

NICKY: And we go on the streets.

JACK: If it is going to be cardboard boxes under the arches, then at least we've got some nice recipes we could dream about.

TIM: I tell you something, if this nightmare were ever to come true and I was going to face the worst with anybody, I'd like to face it with you lot.

JACK: *(Cynically)* Ahh.

TIM: I'm serious. Without getting soppy, I believe we'd be able to create something else together if we had to.

GLORIA: That's true. In fact, before we even get to that point I reckon we could create some other stuff anyway.

NICKY: Like what?

JACK: Recipes for down-and-outs.

TIM: Budget food for street bums?

NICKY: Nutritional facts about eating cardboard?

GLORIA: Surviving on pet food?

General laughter.

JACK: Part of my nightmare is being taken over by another company, being assimilated, you know like the Borg in *Star Trek*.

TIM: Seriously, perhaps we should combine forces with another competitor? That's not a bad idea.

GLORIA: It's worth thinking about, Tim.

At this point we freeze the drama and hear from each of the team members individually, as if they're talking to the Big Brother *camera:*

GLORIA: Funny really. Now we've had a good laugh contemplating the break-up of everything, it's allowed me to face my worst fears. And also see the strength in the team. The reality is, I know we'll survive. We just need to keep positive and be more creative.

NICKY: You know, something happened when Tim said about the worst-case scenario. I hate confronting things like that. But doing it together was a bit therapeutic. It certainly seemed to take some of the fear out of the situation.

TIM: We came up with a few good ideas there. Also, I'm glad we faced the worst together. A problem shared and all that.

JACK: I've always felt the team was more than just a bunch of people working together. Facing the worst made me realize that. I think it's helped strengthen our resolve and sense of community.

Considering the worst that could happen allows the team to:

★   Prepare for a poor future and make contingency plans.
★   Share the worrying, so that it's not just the leader who holds the problem.
★   Build a sense of interdependence and teamworking.
★   Produce creative solutions.

In which Helena has a dramatic dream

On the journey home after an evening at the theatre, Helena finds herself daydreaming. She is imagining what it would be like if her own working world were on a stage. She sees herself sitting in the auditorium watching a drama taking place on stage. It's her working life, and it isn't very exciting. She notices that she keeps seeing people coming in and interrupting her with trivial matters. She gets distracted and is unable to focus on the important issues the business needs. Also, she feels totally unsupported. There are people around her, but they are somehow lifeless. It's as if they're on auto-pilot, simply going through the motions.

Suddenly she 'comes to' with a shudder. 'Is this how it's going to be for the next however many years? Must my existence be one long battle for space to think, to focus, to deal with what really matters? No way!' she says to herself in response to this mental drama.

So she sets herself the task of imagining how she would ideally like her work life to be. She decides to start an entirely different dream, to create a new drama.

Helena pictures walking into the office and feeling really positive about the day ahead of her. What would have to change in order to make that happen? She lets her imagination flow and sees herself surrounded by supportive colleagues who share her enthusiasm for the job. People don't keep running to her for decisions. Instead of pestering her for advice all the time, they act on their own initiative. They only consult her when it's a major decision. Because of this, she has more time to think strategically, and in her mind's eye she sees a scene of her sitting on a sofa brainstorming with a couple of others in her team. In fact all the surroundings are different. There are large pot plants, the area has been painted in bright colours, there are paintings on the walls and other sofas and easy chairs in the coffee area.

Helena starts to get excited by the drama she is creating in her mind. Running through it a few more times, she finds herself adding other details and clarifying the changes she wants. By the time she's finished, she has a very clear vision for an improved drama. Now all she has to do is make it happen!

Helena used a mental drama to uncover a vision of what she wanted.

★   Our minds are well equipped to create a mental drama and play with it.
★   Vision encourages us to influence the future.
★   In your mind, create the performance as it is now and make it come alive as if you were watching it on stage – the people, places, situations, feelings.
★   Give yourself permission to create the drama as you would like it to be.
★   Embroider and elaborate the results, pile on the details.
★   Watch this ideal drama unfold lots of times and enjoy the show.
★   Finally, what will it take to bring this drama to life?

In which executive team members use a technique to give them insight

RONALD: Let me summarize. What's on the table is a proposal to invest in a client relations management system, CRM for short. We can't go on with this downturn in new contracts. The all-singing, all-dancing system will do everything you and your people in client relations will need, Dot. I know it's a big chunk of the budget, Gina, but it's an investment in the future. We've gone round the houses long enough. Are we agreed or not?

DOT: I'm all for getting better information on our clients, so I'm not against a CRM system. I certainly think we need to invest money in something, but I'm not convinced that technology is the solution.

GINA: You'd better be sure. I'm not authorising this level of spend unless you're 100 per cent behind it.

RONALD: Here we go again! I'm telling you as head of IT that this CRM system checks out, it will do what it's meant to do and more.

JAY: Let's step back a bit. It's easy in these situations to get carried away by the rush to do something. We need more insight into the issues. Let's use that 'observe, perceive and wonder' technique and see if that sheds any more light on the situation. Agreed?

ALL: OK.

JAY: We'll start with the facts. What do we actually observe to be the problem?

GINA: Revenue is down because sales are down.

RONALD: So people need a better system to support them in getting more sales.

JAY: Hang on a minute. That's not an observation. You've jumped straight into fix-it mode. Let's stick to the facts for now. What do we observe to be the reality at the moment?

RONALD: Fair enough. I observe – because people have told me this – that they feel unsupported in selling by the present system. They say they don't have enough information when they talk to clients. That's a fact.

DOT: That's right. But another fact is that most of our extra revenue comes from existing clients, ones where we already have a good relationship and a proven track record.

GINA: Is that a fact or an assumption?

DOT: There's some interpretation, but figures do show that our margins are higher when we get more work from existing clients than pursuing new ones.

JAY: Fine. What other observations are there?

DOT: Our competitors have not necessarily benefited from having expensive CRM systems. I was talking to Miles at Hendersons the other day and he was saying that they had invested a huge amount of money in a new system and their revenue was still falling.

JAY: OK. If we put some of these observations together, what are they telling us? What do we perceive from all this?

GINA: Listen, I don't know that much about client relations. Remember, I'm only an accountant, but it seems to me that there isn't a direct link between investing in CRM and an increase in revenue. If, at the same time, we can bring in more business by focusing on our existing clients, then that's where our attention should be, rather than on systems and technology.

DOT: I'm beginning to believe that the technology might be a bit of a distraction. What's really going on here is our inability to build the sort of relationships with clients that would generate larger contracts.

JAY: Pushing this ahead, very quickly, we've observed, we've perceived, now let's do a bit of wondering.

RONALD: Wondering about what?

JAY: Well, I wonder right now what would happen if we didn't buy a new system at all, but did some work on our existing contact management system. And maybe provided some more training for our relationship managers.

DOT: I suppose I'm wondering what would actually make a difference to the way they behave with clients.

GINA: I wonder what would happen if we involved relationship managers in defining exactly what data support they need. What's the essential information and what would be merely nice to have?

RONALD: Interesting. I actually wonder whether we could do something ourselves rather than buying in a whole new system anyway.

GINA: Certainly a cheaper option.

RONALD: I wonder if that would be enough to meet the need? And I'm also wondering what would happen if I starting this wondering business with my IT team!

The observe/perceive/wonder technique is always a good place to start when making tough decisions. It is also a useful double-checking process to employ when embarking on a risky venture.

By using a simple dramatic method of gaining insight, Jay prevented a rush to a possibly expensive and inappropriate solution.

★ Teams often leap too early to a decision or a solution.

★ Use observe, perceive, wonder to promote time for a rethink.

★ Nail down the facts – does everyone agree on what they are? (Observe)

★ How do people interpret these facts – is there agreement on what they mean? (Perceive)

★ What do people's perceptions provoke – what alternatives do they make people curious about? (Wonder)

DINNER AFTER THE SHOW

> EXECUTIVE: I enjoyed that. A great performance.
>
> PRODUCER: Me too. Ultimately that's what it's all about, isn't it – performance? Does it excite us, inspire us and, most important of all, does it make a difference to us?
>
> EXECUTIVE: You've certainly opened my eyes to how theatre can make a difference to my business life.
>
> PRODUCER: Thanks. As we've discussed, it does have a lot to offer. From how you present to how you manage teams, from how you inspire people to how you stay positive in the most negative situations.
>
> EXECUTIVE: I agree. Theatre in business is clearly a lot more than just a metaphor. It's a whole approach to performance that I never really considered up to now. What's worrying is that you seem to know more about business than I know about the theatre!
>
> PRODUCER: That's not actually true. You know your business better than anyone does and you know what it needs. But if you're after outstanding performance, you can't afford to neglect any resource that really works.
>
> EXECUTIVE: No, you're right. Life's too short.
>
> PRODUCER: It's certainly too short to waste our time being involved in pedestrian enterprises that have no meaning for us. There is an alternative.
>
> EXECUTIVE: Always. *(Lifting his glass)* Here's to dramatic success.
>
> PRODUCER: *(Lifting hers)* Dramatic success!

INDEX

MAYNARD
LEIGH
ASSOCIATES

UNLOCKING PEOPLE'S POTENTIAL

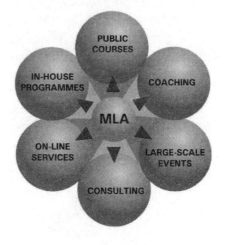

Maynard Leigh Associates
Marvic House
Bishops Road
London Sw6 7AD

e mail info@maynardleigh.co.uk
020 7385 2588
visit us at: www.maynardleigh.co.uk